Perfect Love

Perfect Love

by
John MacArthur, Jr.

MOODY PRESS
CHICAGO

Library of Congress Cataloging-in-Publication Data

MacArthur, John F.
  Perfect love.

  (John MacArthur's Bible studies)
    1. Bible. N.T. Corinthians, 1st XIII, 1-7—
Criticism, interpretation, etc. I. Title. II. Series:
MacArthur, John F. Bible studies.
BS2675.2.M29 1983   227'.206   85-28486
ISBN: 0-8024-5110-1 (pbk.)

1 2 3 4 5 6 7 Printing/GB/90 98 88 87 86 85

Printed in the United States of America

Contents

CHAPTER   PAGE

1. Languages Without Love   5
   Tape GC 1862—1 Cor. 13:1

2. The Prominence of Love   25
   Tape GC 1863—1 Cor. 13:1-3

3. The Qualities of True Love—Part 1   45
   Tape GC 1864—1 Cor. 13:4*a-c*

4. The Qualities of True Love—Part 2   61
   Tape GC 1865—1 Cor. 13:4*d*-5*c*

5. The Qualities of True Love—Part 3   79
   Tape GC 1866—1 Cor. 13:5*c*-6

6. The Qualities of True Love—Part 4   96
   Tape GC 1867—1 Cor. 13:7

1
Languages Without Love

Outline

Introduction
A. The Chapter of Love
    1. Its characteristic style
    2. Its context
    3. Its content
B. The Fruit of Love
C. The Definition of Love
    1. *Agapē* is not
        a) Romantic or sexual love
        b) Emotional love
        c) Ecumenical love
        d) Charity
    2. *Agapē* is
        a) John 3:16
        b) John 13:1, 4-5, 34
        c) John 15:9-10*a*, 13
        d) John 21:15-19
        e) 1 John 4:9-11

Lesson
I. The Prominence of Love
    A. Languages Without Love Are Nothing
        1. The definition of tongues
            a) The tongues of men
               (1) The first occurrence of tongues
               (2) The reasons known languages are in view
            b) The tongues of angels
               (1) No mention elsewhere in Scripture
               (2) Paul's hyperbolic usage
        2. The primary purpose of tongues

Introduction

A. The Chapter of Love

The thirteenth chapter of 1 Corinthians is probably one that you recognize. In fact, if you've been a Christian for any length of time,

5

you probably have a great deal of affection and love for this chapter because of the tremendous impact that it has on the greatest thing in all the world—the subject of love.

Some people have said that this chapter is the greatest, strongest, and deepest thing that the apostle Paul ever penned. It has been called "the hymn of love," "a lyrical interpretation of the Sermon on the Mount," and "the Beatitudes set to music." It is a dramatic chapter. Studying it is almost like taking apart a flower. When the flower is apart, it's not as beautiful as it was before dissection, but it must be done to see the intricacy of God's design. So let's become spiritual botanists for a while and dissect 1 Corinthians 13. Then we will be able to understand the beauties hidden beneath its surface.

1. Its characteristic style

The exciting thing about this chapter is that it is a breath of fresh air in the middle of such a problem-oriented book. First Corinthians is negative in many ways. Paul attacks the Corinthian assembly for all of their misconduct and immorality and their failure to acquiesce to those principles that God has given for their blessing. But all of those issues are set aside in chapter 13 as Paul flies on wings, as it were, interpreting and sharing his Holy Spirit-given inspiration on love.

I can imagine that Paul's amanuensis (or secretary) must have done a double take and looked into his face as he began to dictate chapter 13 because of its dramatic change. It's lyrical and rhetorical—totally different from the rest of the book. He had been plodding through problem after problem with deep reasoning and carefully worded arguments, explanations, and warnings. But all of a sudden, he hits the rhythm of chapter 13, and his words begin to sing. It's like a beautiful gem in a setting. The setting may be attractive, but the gem is what makes the setting. So it is with the thirteenth chapter of 1 Corinthians. It is a gem in the setting of the whole letter.

2. Its context

This particular chapter has been treated with a sense of uniqueness—and rightly so. It's been pulled out, isolated, and preached on as if it were an entity in itself—dropped out of heaven without any connection to anything else. However, the real power of this chapter is found when you study it in its context. This chapter wouldn't mean as much to you if I just pulled it out of its context and taught it. Of course, I feel that way about every chapter in the Bible. However, I particularly feel it applies to this chapter, because I think it gets abused along that line so very frequently. People just pull it out and teach it. Unfortunately, they miss its power, which only comes when it's tied together with the rest of the book—particularly chapters 12 and 14.

First Corinthians 13 is in the middle of a section on spiritual gifts. In chapter 12 Paul discusses the endowments of the gifts—the receiving of the gifts and the way God has put them together in the church so that it can function. Chapter 14 is the proper exercise of the gifts—how to do it and how not to do it. And right in the middle is the proper energy, the proper motive, the proper power, the proper atmosphere, and the proper environment in which the gifts operate—love. It's part of the more excellent way.

3. Its content

In chapter 12, Paul gives the Corinthians all the basics about spiritual gifts. He tells them that since God put the gifts in the church, they were to be content and not to feel inadequate, jealous, and envious if they didn't have a showy gift. And on the other hand, if they did have a showy gift, they were not to be proud, selfish, self-seeking, and boastful.

The Greek rendering of verse 31 says, "Instead of accepting what God has given, you are coveting the showy gifts." It's in the indicative case, not in the imperative. Paul said, "You are continuing to covet the showy gifts. But I show unto you 'a more excellent way.' " In other words, a more excellent way than coveting the showy gift is to be content with the one you have. A more excellent way than lording it over somebody or being proud because you happen to have the gift of speaking, or teaching, or languages is to be loving. That's what he talks about in chapter 13 as he describes, in beautiful language, the more excellent way of love. The Corinthian church had the gifts, as well as a lot of activity. But without love it wasn't excellent. Rather, it was counterfeit. They were selfish and self-seeking, and operating in the flesh.

Chapter 13, then, sums up the more excellent way. Neither conflict, nor struggle, nor self-seeking, nor pride, nor envy, nor jealousy have a place in the Body of Christ—only love.

B. The Fruit of Love

As we talk about love, we're getting into the very heart of Paul's view of spiritual life. Love is basic. We could spend weeks and weeks and weeks on that subject alone. However, what Paul is saying here is this: The truly spiritual life is the only life in which spiritual gifts can truly operate. And the truly spiritual life is not controlled by the gifts of the Spirit, it is controlled by the fruit of the Spirit. Do you understand that? The Corinthians had all the gifts of the Spirit but none of the fruit of the Spirit.

According to Galatians 5:22-23, the fruit of the Spirit is "love, joy, peace, long-suffering, gentleness, goodness, faith, meekness, self-control." If you don't have the fruit of the Spirit, then the gifts of the Spirit are functioning in the flesh. It's a simple process. When the believer walks in the Spirit, the fruit of the Spirit is produced. Out of the fruit of the Spirit come the gifts of the Spirit operating in the power of the Spirit.

Now it's possible that love is the fruit of the Spirit and the rest of those words just describe love in all its dimensions. Love is certainly the greatest, according to 1 Corinthians 13:13, where Paul says, "The greatest of these is love." If there's no love, then what is being done is being done without the fruit of the Spirit. And if it's being done without the fruit of the Spirit, it's being done without the Spirit. It's in the flesh—fleshly, carnal, counterfeit. Even though the Corinthians had all the gifts of the Spirit, they were exercising their gifts in the flesh without the fruit of the Spirit. So Paul says, "When it all gets done, you won't have anything."

Look at the first three verses of chapter 13, and change the word *though* to *if*. The Greek word *ean* is better translated "if." It reads like this: "[If] I speak with the [languages] of men and of angels, and have not love, I am become as sounding bronze, or a tinkling cymbal. And [if] I have the gift of prophecy, and understand all mysteries, and all knowledge; and [if] I have all faith, so that I could remove mountains, and have not love, I am anothing. And [if] I bestow all my goods to feed the poor, and [if] I give my body to be burned, and have not love, it profiteth me nothing." In other words, Paul says, "All of the gifts of the Spirit and all of the activities mean nothing without the fruit of the Spirit—love." Love has to be the driving force and the motive for everything in the life of the believer. You see, it's possible to have the gifts of the Spirit without spirituality. Just having a spiritual gift doesn't make you spiritual. You can either function in the energy of your flesh as you counterfeit the gifts, or you can function in the power of the Spirit. But without the fruit of the Spirit, your work is in the flesh.

The Corinthians, then, were prophesying, speaking in languages, and supposedly healing people. However, their lack of love gave evidence that their flesh was operating instead of the Spirit. Consequently, their works were counterfeit. I think it's tremendously important for us to understand that God doesn't want us doing our own thing in our own power—a principle that is unfolded in this chapter.

C. The Definition of Love

Love is the more excellent way. However, in talking about the word *love,* I think we'd better define it, since our world doesn't have the foggiest idea what it means. The word in the Greek is *agapē,* which is the most grandiose concept of love. Agape is the highest level of love—the love that is associated with God. Agape is the term used in 1 Corinthians 13. So the question is, What does it mean? Well, first let me tell you what it doesn't mean.

1. Agape is not

8

a) Romantic or sexual love

The word *love,* as it appears in the Word of God, never means romantic or sexual love. The Greeks had a word for that (*erōs*), but it never appears in the New Testament. For example, when it says in Ephesians 5, "Husbands, love your wives" (v. 25*a*), it isn't talking about romance. Yet how many sermons have you heard, or how many books have you read, where someone says, "Husbands, love your wives," and then gives illustrations about opening the car door, buying flowers, and feeling romantic? That isn't what it's talking about.

So, agape never refers to romance or sex. Second, biblical love never means:

b) Emotional love

Paul's not talking about a tingly sensation or sentimentalism. He's not saying, "The greatest of these is sentimentality." That, too, is not scriptural love.

Third, the word *love,* as it appears in the Bible, never means:

c) Ecumenical love

Biblical love is never a friendly spirit of tolerance and brotherhood toward others, without any thought of convictions. In other words, when people say, "Well, it doesn't matter what anybody believes, as long as there's some kind of common ground. We just have to love them all," they don't understand the biblical meaning of love.

Recently, there was a prayer meeting where both Christian and non-Christian people were in attendance. When the director of this meeting, who happened to be a Christian, was asked on what basis they got together, he said, "Oh, on the basis of love." "Well, they don't even believe the truth of the gospel!" the inquirer replied. "No, we don't agree on that, but we do agree on prayer. We all pray—that's our common ground. Even if we don't pray to the same person, I guess it's OK." But you see, that kind of friendly spirit of tolerance and brotherhood, without any thought of conviction or doctrine, isn't what the Bible is talking about.

Further, biblical love cannot be defined as:

d) Charity

Unfortunately, the King James translators used the word *charity* instead of the word *love* in 1 Corinthians 13. But that is too narrow a definition. Paul is not talking about giving your nickel to the United Fund. That isn't the basic thrust of the chapter or of the term.

So, if love isn't romantic, or sexual, or emotional, or the friendly spirit of ecumenical tolerance, or charity, what in the world is it? What is love? Well, I'll show you what it is biblically.

2. Agape is

a) John 3:16

Now see if any of the previous definitions fit this verse: "For God so loved the world . . . that He felt romantic about it . . . that He got a tingly sensation down His spine . . . that He had a friendly spirit of tolerance and brotherhood no matter what they believed . . . that He gave to the United Fund." Do any of those definitions of love fit? No! What does the verse say? "For God so loved the world, that He gave His only begotten son." What is love, then? Love is an act of self-sacrifice, not a feeling. Biblically, this is seen again and again. Love is an act of self-sacrifice. There's no such thing as agape without action. There's no such thing as the feeling, or the emotion, or the sensation of agape. It is an action. Now the sensation may or may not be there, but the action is always there.

b) John 13:1, 4-5, 34

In John 13:1, Jesus is meeting with His disciples for the last time. At the end of the verse, John says of Jesus, "Having loved his own who were in the world, he loved them unto the end." The Greek literally says, "He loved them to perfection." In other words, He loved them to the limits of love. He loved them as far as love could go. In verses 4-5, we see the extent of Jesus' love for the disciples: "He riseth from supper, and laid aside his garments, and took a towel, and girded himself. After that he poureth water into a basin, and began to wash the disciples' feet, and to wipe them with the towel with which he was girded." He loved them, and His love took action. What kind of action? He washed their dirty feet while they sat around and argued about who was going to be the greatest in the kingdom and about who was going to sit next to Jesus in the Millennium. They weren't about to wash each other's feet, so Jesus stooped and did it. Why? Because He loved them.

At the end of the same chapter, this concept really comes home hard. In verse 34 He says, "A new commandment I give unto you, that ye love one another." How? "As I have loved you." How had He just loved them? By washing their feet. You see, it's the same thing that He's asking of us. Love is an act of self-sacrifice. It is an act of sacrificial giving. It's washing feet. It's God giving His Son.

c) John 15:9-10*a*, 13

In John 15:9 Jesus says, "As the Father hath loved me, so have I loved you; continue ye in my love." How had He loved them? By coming into the world and dying for them.

10

Now look at verse 10*a*: "If ye keep my commandments, ye shall abide in my love." In other words, love toward God is the act of sacrificing my will to do His will. That's it. Love is an act of self-sacrifice.

Verse 13 gives us the supreme example: "Greater love hath no man than this." In other words, here is the greatest definition of love that has ever been given—"that a man lay down his life for his friends." The greatest definition of love is an act of supreme self-sacrifice. That's the way it always appears in Scripture.

d) John 21:15-19

Basically, Jesus told Peter, "If you love Me, then follow Me. But it will cost you your life." Love is self-sacrifice.

e) 1 John 4:9-11

"In this way manifested the love of God toward us, that God sent his only begotten Son into the world, that we might live through him. Herein is love, not that we loved God, but that he loved us, and sent his Son to be the propitiation for our sins. Beloved, if God so loved us, we ought also to love one another." In other words, God's love is demonstrated in an act of self-sacrifice—and so is ours.

Now, when we talk about love, that's what we're talking about. It is an act of self-sacrifice. It is humility. It is meeting needs and doing what God wants us to do. There's no self-seeking, pride, selfishness, self-glory, or vanity in love.

The Only Legitimate Reason to Exercise Your Spiritual Gifts

Did you know that we can minister our gifts in pride? I can preach for fame, or success, or glory, or prestige. I can even preach to be accepted. You can minister your gift for the same reasons, too. You can minister your gift because of peer pressure, or to get out from under a divine obligation that's bugging you, or to have somebody pat you on your spiritual back and tell you how great you are. So can I.

There are myriad other reasons or motives that we could have for ministering our spiritual gifts, but there's only one that's legitimate—the sacrifice of ourselves to the will of God and the sacrifice of our lives to the needs of our brothers and sisters. That's the only legitimate reason. Nothing else matters. Any other reason adds up to zero. Without sacrificial service, you are nothing but noise—a banging gong and a clanging cymbal.

Now let's go back to 1 Corinthians 13. Paul is calling on these people to love, and saying, "Forget yourself." After he told the Philippians to have the same love for one another (2:2), he went on to define that love: "Let each esteem others better than themselves. Look not every man on his own things, but every man also on the things of others. Let this mind be in you, which was also in Christ Jesus, who, being in the form of God, thought it not robbery to be equal with God . . . and, being found in fashion as a man, he humbled himself and became obedient unto death, even the death of the cross" (2:3b-6, 8). Now that's love—an act of humble service and self-sacrifice. And that is exactly what the Corinthian church needed.

The Corinthians didn't have a doctrinal problem. Do you realize that Paul doesn't even mention any significant doctrine until he gets to the fifteenth chapter, when he talks about resurrection? Up until that point, he didn't have to straighten out their doctrine as he did with the Colossians, the Galatians, and others. The Corinthians knew their doctrine; they just didn't have love.

Love is such a desperately needed thing. Karl Menninger of the Menninger Clinic, one of the leading figures in American psychiatry, says, "Love is the medicine for our sick old world. If people can learn to give and receive love, they will usually recover from their physical or mental illness." The problem is, people can't learn to receive or give love because they don't even know how to define it. They think it's nothing more than a warm feeling.

Now, as we look at this chapter on love, we're going to see some very poignant things. This chapter falls into four parts: The Prominence of Love (vv. 1-3), The Properties of Love (vv. 4-7), The Permanence of Love (vv. 8-12), and The Preeminence of Love (v. 13).

Lesson

I. The Prominence of Love (vv. 1-3)

Paul starts out this chapter by trying to show the Corinthians how important love is and how they were wasting their time. Remember what John says to the church at Ephesus in Revelation 2? "You have this and you have that, and you do this and you do that." Then in verse 4, he says, "Nevertheless, I have somewhat against thee, because thou hast left thy first love." They had all the activity without any love, so it was all meaningless. Consequently, the church at Ephesus was removed from the face of the earth—never to be replaced. The candlestick was taken away.

Now keep in mind, as we study these three verses, that Paul is using hyperbole to make his point. He exaggerates and pushes everything to its ultimate limit. For example, in verse 1 he says, in effect, "If I could talk angel talk, it wouldn't matter without love." Then in verses 2-3 he says, "If I knew all mysteries and all knowledge, and had all faith, and bestowed all my goods to feed the poor, and gave my body to be burned, without love it wouldn't matter." In other words, Paul gave the extremes and pushed everything to its limit to make his point that it doesn't matter what you do, what you know, or how far you go unless love is the motive. Without love, it's all nothing.

A. Languages Without Love Are Nothing (v. 1)

"[If] I speak with the [languages] of men and of angels, and have not love, I am become as sounding bronze, or a tinkling cymbal."

Notice that Paul is talking in the first person. That's a good thing to do when you're teaching, so that you identify yourself as one who is also a sinner saved by grace and able to fall into any sin that anybody else could fall into. Paul said, "I could use my gift of languages without love, just like you." Incidentally, Paul did have that gift. In 14:18, he said, "I thank my God, I speak with [languages] more than ye all." So he said, "I could have the languages of men, and even talk angel talk. But if I didn't have love, I would become as sounding bronze and a tinkling cymbal."

1. The definition of tongues

Notice the phrase "speak with the tongues of men and of angels." In the first place, I like to translate the word there "languages," not "tongues," because that quickly eliminates some needless confusion. The word "tongues" is the word for languages, so we can translate it that way. The gift of languages, then, is the same as what people today call the gift of tongues.

a) The tongues of men

What does it mean to speak with the languages of men? What is the gift of languages? The New Testament is exceedingly clear on what this gift was. There isn't any doubt about it. And as you study the Word of God, you'll find that it's relatively simple to ascertain its definition. Let me take you to its first occurrence in Acts, chapter 2, to see what it is and to get a basic definition.

(1) The first occurrence of tongues

In Acts 2:1, we find that the Day of Pentecost has arrived—a great feast time following the Passover, when Jerusalem was loaded with people who had come on a pilgrimage to the festivals: "And when the day of Pentecost was fully come, they were all with one accord in one place." One hundred twenty disciples were gathered (Acts 1:15), waiting for the promised Holy Spirit to come. The church was about to be born. In verse 2-4 we read: "And suddenly there came a sound from heaven like a rushing mighty wind, and it filled all the house where they were sitting. And there appeared unto them cloven tongues as of fire, and it sat upon each of them. And they were all filled with the Holy Spirit, and began to speak with other tongues [lit., languages], as the Spirit gave them utterance." The Holy Spirit descended, baptized the believers into the Body, moved into their lives, and filled them. And to give evidence of that, a marvelous miracle took place, as they began to speak in other languages under the enabling of the Holy Spirit.

The word translated "tongues" is the Greek word *glōssa*—the normal Greek word for language. In other words, they spoke with other languages. Now there are some people today who say that the gift of tongues is ecstatic babble—a prayer language. I've heard many who say that the gift of tongues is their own private language. But let's look into this and see if that is, in fact, true or not true. When they began to speak with other tongues (or languages) in verse 4, was it babble or not?

Well, that's an easy question to answer if you just continue reading this passage. Let's start at verse 5. "And there were dwelling at Jerusalem Jews, devout men, out of every nation under heaven. Now when this was noised abroad, the multitude came together and were confounded, because every man heard them speak in his own language." There's no question about the fact that the tongues of verse 4 were languages. They had to be. Why? Because "every man heard them speak in his own language."

Further, verse 7 tells us that "they were all amazed and marveled, saying one to another, Behold, are not all these who speak Galileans?" Now the Galileans were considered to be the hayseeds or the hicks of that time. They weren't connected to the highfalutin, educated people of Jerusalem. So the people must have thought, "How could these Galileans be linguists? They don't even have schools up there to teach this stuff." Consequently, they were amazed to hear their own particular tongue, or language, being spoken (v. 8).

What languages did they speak? They're listed in verses 9-11. First he starts in the east with the "Parthians, and Medes, and Elamites, and the dwellers in Mesopotamia." Then he goes west to "Judea," north to "Cappadocia . . . Pontus, and Asia, Phrygia, and Pamphylia in Egypt," and south to "the parts of Libya about Cyrene." Then he gets very general by mentioning the "sojourners of Rome, both Jews and proselytes, Cretans and Arabians." And according to the end of verse 11, they all heard, in their own languages, "the wonderful works of God."

Let me ask you this: How would they have know the

disciples were proclaiming the wonderful works of God if it wasn't being done in a known language—particularly their own language? Well, the fact that they knew what the disciples were saying, and that they recognized their own languages, proves that the disciples were speaking in known languages—not babble or ecstatic speech. The gift of tongues was not a private gift that they exercised in their closets all by themselves. It referred to the use of bona fide human languages.

(2) The reasons known languages are in view

Now, I want to show you that according to the Bible the gift of languages was always languages and never anything else. This is an important point for you to understand.

(a) The Greek word *glōssa* primarily means "human language" when used in Scripture

The word *glōssa,* from which we get *glossolalia,* is a word that found its way into our English language without being translated. It means "tongue." Biblically, however, *glōssa* always means "human language" in the New Testament. And of the thirty times it appears in the Greek translation of the Old Testament (the Septuagint), its meaning is "normal, bona fide, human language" in all but two cases: Isaiah 29:24 and Isaiah 32:4. And in those verses, it doesn't refer to ecstatic speech or pagan babble; it simply means "a stammering" or "a stuttering." So the normal usage of *glōssa* in Scripture is to refer to intelligent, normal, human language. That's the way it appears in Acts 2, because that's its normal meaning.

(b) The Greek word *dialektos,* from which we get the English word *dialect,* is used in Acts 2:6 and 8

Some of the people in the crowd at Pentecost heard God's message proclaimed in their own language, and some of them heard it in their own dialect (which is a subgroup of a language). The disciples were speaking in languages and dialects. That's very clear, according to Acts 2. Now those classifications would never be used to describe babble or ecstatic speech, only normal languages and dialects known to the people who heard.

(c) The gift of tongues in Acts 2 is the same throughout the book of Acts

People say, "Yes, we agree that languages are mentioned in Acts 2. But the meaning changes later on in

15

Acts." Well, that's not true. It doesn't change. Look at Acts 10:44-46a: "While Peter yet spoke these words, the Holy Spirit fell on all them who heard the word. And they of the circumcision who believed were astonished, as many as came with Peter, because on the Gentiles also was poured out the gift of the Holy Spirit. For they heard them speak with tongues [languages]." Now, you can't say, "Well by now, *glōssa* means babble." No. It means languages. It's the same word.

Further, look at Acts 11:15-17a. Peter, reporting back to Jerusalem of the incident that occurred in Acts 10, says, "And as I began to speak [in Cornelius's house], the Holy Spirit fell on them, as on us at the beginning. Then remembered I the word of the Lord, how he said, John indeed baptized with water; but ye shall be baptized with the Holy Spirit. Forasmuch, then, as God gave them the same gift as He did unto us." In other words, Peter said, "They received the same thing we received at Pentecost." What did they receive? Languages. It had to be the same thing that they experienced in Acts 2.

In Acts 19:6 we find a similar situation: "And when Paul had laid his hands upon them, the Holy Spirit came on them, and they spoke with tongues [Gk., *glōssa,* "languages"]." The same term means the same thing in the same book. There's no reason to think it means babble.

So throughout the book of Acts, *glōssa* consistently refers to normal human language. And the point is this: Once it happened in Jerusalem on the Day of Pentecost, the Jews said, "We received the Holy Spirit in this marvelous way." But God responded, later on in the book of Acts, by showing the Jews that the Gentiles received the same Holy Spirit and the same corresponding gift of languages. That's how God put the church together. Furthermore, in Acts 19, the disciples of John the Baptist experienced the exact same thing. The Lord gave all the groups the same experience, to weld the whole church into one unit. Therefore, *glōssa* must be translated the same way throughout the book of Acts.

(*d*) The word "interpretation" (Gk., *hermeneuō*) in 1 Corinthians 12:10, is the normative word for translating languages

16

The Greek word *hermeneuō* can't be referring to the interpretation of babble, because babble is not a language. What people today have done is to say that the purpose of the gift of interpretation is to translate someone's babble. But the Greek word refers to taking something in one language and putting it into its equivalent in another known language. And you can't translate babble. So, the very word that is used demands that a known language be in view.

(e) The word "unknown" in the phrase "unknown tongue" throughout 1 Corinthians 14, was added by the King James translators and is not in the original

(f) First Corinthians 12:10 mentions different "kinds" of tongues

The word "kinds" is the Greek word *genos,* from which we get our English word *genus.* It means "a family, group, race, or nation." You can't say there are kinds and races and classes and groups and families of babble or ecstatic speech. Why? Because there aren't any. However, there are language families, aren't there? Any linguist is familiar with the phrase "language families." There are national languages and there are racial languages. So, the term "kinds" fits languages, not babble.

(g) First Corinthians 14:21 indicates that tongues were a foreign language given as a sign to unbelieving Israel

Paul referred to Isaiah 28:11-12 when he said, "In the law it is written, With men of other tongues and other lips will I speak unto this people; and yet for all that will they not hear me, saith the Lord." Isaiah predicted that men of other languages would speak to Israel. Do you know who fulfilled that? The Assyrians. Do you know what they spoke? Assyrian. So the prophecy had reference to a known language—Assyrian spoken by Assyrians. That is the standard. Paul, then, goes on to say, in verse 22, that tongues are for a sign—not to believers, but to unbelieving Israel. And since the tongues spoken of in Isaiah 28 is a legitimate language, the tongues in 1 Corinthians 14 must be the same.

(h) According to 1 Corinthians 14:7-8, tongues had to have grammatical structure

In 14:7-8 Paul says, "And even things without life, giving sound, whether flute or harp, except they give a distinction in the sounds, how shall it be known what is piped or harped? For if the trumpet give an

17

uncertain sound, who shall prepare himself to the battle?" Can you imagine what would have happened when the U.S. Cavalry went out to fight the Indians, if the bugler blew just any tune he wanted to? The men wouldn't know what to do. The bugler had to blow a specific series of notes to communicate specific instructions, such as "Hit the horses, guys" or "It's time to get up." The soldiers had to know what each series of notes meant. It had to have structure and distinction. And that's the point Paul is trying to make. Language has to have structural distinction to make sense. It can't just be pagan babble."

(i) The effectiveness of the sign of the gift of languages depended upon its difference from the ecstatic babble of pagan worship

The Corinthians had allowed babble and strange ecstatic languages into their church—counterfeiting the true gift of languages. In fact, their ecstasy was turning their worship service into an orgy. Look at 1 Corinthians 14:23: "If, therefore, the whole church be come together into one place, and all speak with tongues [or "languages"], and there come in those that are unlearned, or unbelievers, will they not say that ye are mad?" In other words, Paul says, "If you have all of this wild hysteria going on, with everybody up doing his own thing, you're going to have problems, because unbelieving people are going to think you're nuts. It's not going to have any effect on them." Why? Because the amazement element, for non-Christian Jews attending their services, depended upon the fact that real languages were spoken and then translated miraculously. That would obviously be seen as a sign from God. In other words, the effectiveness of the sign of the gift of languages depended upon its difference from the ecstatic babble that they were so used to in the pagan worship of Corinth. So, in the Corinthian assembly, the genuine gift of languages was a true language with a true translation. That was the miracle. If all an unbeliever heard was babble, he wouldn't be able to say anything except, "This is just the same old pagan hysteria."

So, in terms of a definition, the gift of tongues is a Spirit-given ability to speak a foreign language.

18

Are the tongues of today the same as the New Testament gift of tongues?

When you compare the proper definition of the gift of tongues with what is going on today, there are some definite problems. I've read books that tell you how to get your own prayer language—one that's like nobody else's. Or if you want, you can share somebody else's prayer language when you're first learning, until you develop your own. And on and on it goes. Modern tongues are nothing more than ecstatic babble without structure or grammar. And they definitely cannot be considered actual languages. They just don't fit the New Testament definition of the gift of tongues.

William Samarin, Ph.D. in linguistics and professor of linguistics at the University of Toronto, says this: "Over a period of five years I have taken part in meetings in Italy, Holland, Jamaica, Canada and the United States. I have observed old-fashioned Pentecostals and neo-Pentecostals. I have been in small meetings in private homes as well as in mammoth public meetings. I have seen such different cultural settings as are found among Puerto Ricans of the Bronx, the snake handlers of the Appalachians and the Russian Molakans of Los Angeles . . . I have interviewed tongue speakers, and tape recorded and analyzed countless samples of Tongues. In every case, glossolalia turns out to be linguistic nonsense. In spite of superficial similarities, glossolalia is fundamentally not language." (See William Samarin, *Tongues of Men and Angels* [New York: Macmillan, 1972], pp. 103-128, for further expansion of that claim.)

If a man with a Ph.D. in linguistics does a study of modern tongues and determines that what we're hearing today is not language, then it's not what the Bible says the gift is. And I would also hasten to add, that even if a real language is spoken occasionally, you'd better be careful. Why? Because demons are multi-lingual and there are many counterfeits.

b) The tongues of angels

Many people will admit that 1 Corinthians 13:1 refers to legitimate languages of men, but they claim that "the tongues of . . . angels" refers to an angelic, private, devotional language that is beyond the human. However, there are some problems with that definition of angel talk. For example:

(1) No mention elsewhere in Scripture

If you're going to make the angel talk of 1 Corinthians 13:1 the gift of tongues, you're going to have to force it into this verse, because it's nowhere else in the entire

Bible. There is no precedent anywhere. In fact, anytime an angel ever communicated with a man, he communicated in normal human language.

The only kind of language we know about, apart from human language, is the language between the Holy Spirit and the Father recorded in Romans 8. However, that language is made up of "groanings which cannot be uttered" (v. 26*b*). It is a silent language. You say, "Do you think the angels speak a silent language?" Well, angels are ministering spirits (Heb. 1:7), and spirits don't have mouths or vocal chords. You say, "Well, how do they communicate?" I don't know how they communicate, but there is no mention anywhere else in the Bible of an angel language.

(2) Paul's hyperbolic usage

"What is Paul saying?" you ask. Well, he's *not* stating a factual reality. He is using hyperbole—exaggeration to make a point. This is part of his push-to-the-limits argument that appears throughout verses 2 and 3 with his use of subjunctive verbs—verbs that indicate a hypothetical situation.

For example, in verse 2 Paul says, "And [if] I . . . understand all mysteries, and all knowledge; and [if] I have all faith, so that I could remove mountains." Now, is all of that possible? Is it possible for Paul to understand all that's ever been revealed by God? No. Is it possible for him to have the knowledge of every single fact in the universe? That's absurd. And if Paul had the kind of faith that could remove mountains, he wouldn't have got sick climbing the mountains from Pamphylia to Phrygia, believe me. He would have just said, "Be removed," and they would have disappeared. He didn't have all faith, all knowledge, or all mysteries. And, believe me, if he didn't have it, I'm a long way from having it.

Do you see what Paul is doing? He's talking in limits and giving hypothetical situations. He is not saying that we can speak the language of angels, any more than we can understand all mysteries or all knowledge, or have all faith. We can't! It is beyond our limits. "But," says Paul, "even if we could, it wouldn't matter without love. It wouldn't mean a thing." Paul's point, then, is this: The gift of tongues, if used without love, is nothing more than noise.

We've seen the definition of tongues, now let's look at:

2. The primary purpose of tongues

You say, "John, what was the primary purpose of tongues?" It was a sign to Israel. The only time it ever had any meaning to a Christian at all was when it was translated. That's the only time. I don't know how people can go into a corner and speak babble and then think they have the gift of tongues. That's not the gift! And furthermore, if the languages aren't interpreted, edification isn't possible. Yet people do just that and claim that it builds them up and strengthens them. In fact, people even claim that their ecstatic babble is their devotional language. However, the Bible doesn't define the gift of tongues that way.

The gift of tongues isn't for personal edification or devotion—it's a sign to Israel of God's turning away from them to the church—the Gentiles. And it wouldn't even matter if you had the gift of tongues if you didn't have love. Even if you could talk angel talk, if you didn't have love, you would be like "sounding bronze, or a tinkling cymbal."

Sounding Bronze or a Tinkling Cymbal

I did some reading to find out what was going on in the pagan worship of Paul's day, and I discovered something very fascinating. In the worship of Cybele and Dionysus, two pagan false gods, there was speaking in ecstatic languages accompanied by "clanging cymbals, smashing gongs, and blaring trumpets" (William Barclay, *The Letters to the Corinthians* [Philadelphia: Westminster, 1956], p. 131). Isn't that amazing? In other words, he is saying to them, "When you go about trying to operate your spiritual gifts in the flesh—no matter how good you are at it, or no matter how far it goes—if love isn't the motive, it's no different than a pagan rite. It's just paganism—pure and simple.

Unless gifts are ministered out of the power of the Spirit, through the fruit of the Spirit, in the energy of the Spirit, and in accordance with the Word of God written by the Spirit, it's just pagan racket—banging gongs, clanging cymbals, and blaring trumpets. It's just paganism within the walls of the church.

Let me carry all of this to its logical end. The best speech on earth from the most gifted orator is nothing but racket, if it's delivered without love. And we may minister our spiritual gifts in the flesh, apart from the Spirit and the love that the Spirit generates. But if we do, it means absolutely nothing. In fact, it's just paganism with Christian terminology. Now, we can't sit in condemnation of people in a movement we disagree with and say that they're the ones that are acting like pagans. Why? Because we act just as pagan when we operate our gifts in the flesh. God help us not to do that. Remember, as we walk in the

Spirit, He produces the fruit. And out of that fruit comes the ministry of the gifts with the blessing of God.

Focusing on the Facts

1. How is chapter 13 different from the rest of 1 Corinthians (see p. 6)?

2. Why is it so important that 1 Corinthians 13 be taught in its immediate context (see pp. 6-7)?

3. First Corinthians 13 is preceded by and followed by a discussion of what important subject (see p. 7)?

4. What is the "more excellent way" that is mentioned in 1 Corinthians 12:31 (see p. 7)?

5. The truly spiritual life is not controlled by the gifts of the Spirit; it is controlled by the _____ of the Spirit (see p. 7).

6. Can spiritual gifts be exercised in the flesh? Explain (see pp. 7-8).

7. What is the key in knowing whether or not you are operating in the flesh or in the Spirit (see p. 8)?

8. What is the Greek word for the highest level of love? What Greek word is used in 1 Corinthians 13 for love (see p. 8)?

9. Biblical love cannot be defined as _____ or _____ love, _____ love, _____ love, or _____ (see p. 9).

10. How is biblical love defined? Give two scriptural references to support this definition (see pp. 10-11)?

11. What are some of the illegitimate reasons for exercising your spiritual gift? What is the only legitimate reason (see p. 11)?

12. Did Paul have to write the Corinthians to clear up major doctrinal problems? Explain (see p. 12).

13. The gift of tongues can also be referred to as the gift of _____. Why is this helpful (see p. 13)?

14. Where is the first occurrence of the gift of languages in the New Testament? Describe the circumstances (see p. 13).

15. What Greek word is translated "tongues"? What is a better translation of this word (see p. 14)?

16. Why must the "tongues" of Acts 2:4 be legitimate languages, according to Acts 2:5-11 (see pp. 15-16)?

17. Why were the people who were present at Pentecost so amazed that the disciples were speaking so many foreign languages (see p. 16)?

18. Why is the latter part of Acts 2:11 so important in determining whether or not the disciples were speaking legitimate languages or ecstatic babble (see pp. 14-15)?

19. What is the primary meaning of the Greek word *glōssa* in Scripture? Does it ever refer to ecstatic speech or pagan blabble (see p. 15)?

20. What common English word comes from the Greek word *dialektos?* Why does the use of this word in Acts 2:6 and 8 support the view that tongues are normal languages (see p. 15)?

21. Is the gift of tongues in Acts 2 the same as the gift of tongues mentioned throughout the book of Acts (see pp. 15-16)?

22. What is the significance of Paul's use of the word "interpretation" in 1 Corinthians 12:10 (see p. 17)?

23. Why doesn't the phrase "unknown tongues," as it is used in 1 Corinthians 14, support the definition of tongues as babble (see p. 17)?

24. Why does the phrase "kinds of tongues" in 1 Corinthians 12:10 support the view that tongues were languages and not babble (see p. 17)?

25. What does 1 Corinthians 14:21-22 indicate about tongues (see p. 17)?

26. What verses in 1 Corinthians 14 show that tongues had to have a grammatical structure (see pp. 17-18)?

27. What happens to the effectiveness of the purpose of the gift of tongues if real languages are not spoken and translated (see p. 18)?

28. Give a simple biblical definition of the gift of tongues. How does this compare with the speaking in tongues that is going on today (see p. 19)?

29. Why can't 1 Corinthians 13:1 be used to support the belief that "the tongues . . . of angels" refers to an angelic, private devotional language that Christians are to engage in (see pp. 19-20)?

30. In 1 Corinthians 13:1-3, is Paul stating factual realities or a hypothetical situation? Support your answer (see p. 20).

31. What is the overall point Paul is trying to make in 1 Corinthians 13:1 (see p. 20)?

32. What was the primary purpose of the gift of tongues? When was the only time it ever had an edifying effect on a Christian (see p. 21)?

33. What is significant about Paul's use of the phrase "sounding bronze, or a tinkling cymbal" (see p. 21)?

Pondering the Principles

1. Take a moment to evaluate whether or not you are exercising your spiritual gift in the power of the Spirit with the motive of love, or if you are selfishly exercising your gift without love in the energy of the flesh. Spend some time in prayer and ask God to make you sensitive to the times when you are attempting to exercise your gift without love.

2. Biblically, love is not an emotion; it is an act—an act of self-sacrifice. Write down some specific ways that you can show love to those in your family and to Christians in your local fellowship. Then ask God to give you opportunities to express that love.

3. The issue of speaking in tongues has been a volatile and divisive issue in the church in recent years. If you believe that speaking in tongues

is still for today, carefully consider the reasons the New Testament gift of tongues had to be legitimate languages (see pp. 15-18), and then ask yourself if that is what is going on today. If you are already convinced that the gift of speaking in tongues was a temporary sign gift that passed away with the apostolic era, consider the following: How should you respond to those who feel you must speak in tongues to be "spiritual"? Are you prepared to show them, biblically, why you believe what you believe? Does loving them mean that you are to overlook their doctrinal error, or does love seek to teach them the truth? Just remember this: The Bible isn't interpreted by experience; experience is interpreted by the Bible.

2
The Prominence of Love

Outline

Introduction
A. Love: Its Confusion in English
B. Love: Its Clarification in Greek
    1. The meaning of agape
    2. The source of agape
C. Love: Its Corruption in Corinth

Review
I. The Prominence of Love
   A. Languages Without Love Are Nothing

Lesson
   B. Prophecy Without Love Is Nothing
      1. The elements of prophecy
      2. The expression of prophecy
      3. The enemies of prophecy
      4. The examples of prophecy
         a) Prophets without love
            (1) Balaam
            (2) Counterfeit prophets
         b) Prophets with love
            (1) Jeremiah
            (2) Paul
   C. Knowledge Without Love Is Nothing
      1. The specifics of knowledge
         a) "All mysteries"
            (1) The mystery of God in human flesh (Col. 2:2-3, 9;
                1 Tim. 3:16)
            (2) The mystery of Christ in us (Col. 1:26-27)
            (3) The mystery of the church as a body (Eph. 3:3-6, 9)
            (4) The mystery of iniquity (2 Thess. 2:7)
         b) "All knowledge"
      2. The superiority of love
   D. Faith Without Love Is Nothing

    1. The gift of faith discussed
       a) Matthew 17:20
       b) Matthew 21:21
    2. The gift of faith defined
 E. Benevolence Without Love Is Nothing
    1. The meaning specified
    2. The motive scrutinized
       a) The improper motives
       b) The proper motive
 F. Martyrdom Without Love Is Nothing
    1. The possible interpretations
       a) Branded to become a slave
       b) Burned to become a martyr
          (1) Future persecution
          (2) Past persecution
          (3) Local illustration
    2. The personal motive

Introduction

A. Love: Its Confusion in English

We've been looking at 1 Corinthians 13 and talking about the subject of love—an important subject to talk about. Unfortunately, in English the word *love* can have many meanings. When people say that they love their car, or their wife, or their dog, or their new dress, they mean different things, don't they? The English language doesn't make this distinction, however. It just uses the same word.

B. Love: Its Clarification in Greek

The Greek language has multiple words that the English language translates *love*. In fact, these different Greek words have absolutely no connection to each other. However, we relate these words because the English word is the same. For example, the Greeks would talk about erotic love, which is the love that we know as a physical attraction between a man and a woman on a sexual level. But the word that they used to refer to that particular emotion (Gk., *erōs*), was not related to their word for love (Gk., *agapē*). They had another Greek word (*philos*) for friendliness—the kind of warm affection that comes when two people become very close, apart from any sexual attraction at all. That, too, is a totally unrelated and different word than the Greek word for love.

1. The meaning of agape

The Greek word that is used in 1 Corinthians 13 for love (*agapē*) is a word that simply means "the ultimate act of self-sacrifice." It is a word that refers to the ultimate act of sacrificing oneself for the good of someone else. In fact, 1 Corinthians 13:1 could easily be translated the following way: "If I

26

speak with the tongues of men and of angels, and have not a spirit of self-sacrifice, I am nothing." Now that would be the essence of the word *love* as it is in the Greek.

I think the spirit of the meaning of agape is indicated by our Lord Jesus when He said, "Love your enemies" (Matt. 5:44*a*). Now what did He mean by that? Well, He went on to say what He meant: "Do good to them that . . . persecute you." That is the essence of the highest kind of love. It is an act of self-sacrificial service toward somebody who does not necessarily care for you emotionally. To love your enemies doesn't mean to feel erotic about them, or to have a wonderful, warm, and happy relationship with them. Those are all impossible. What it *does* mean, however, is to make an act of self-sacrifice on their behalf.

You say, "Why are we to love our enemies and do good to those who persecute us?" Well, continuing on in Matthew 5:45 Jesus says, "That ye may be the sons of your Father, who is in heaven." In other words, love your enemies in the same way that God loved His enemies. And how did God love His enemies? He died on their behalf (Rom. 5:8-10). Love, then, is an act of self-sacrifice toward people who are your enemies. That's the pattern of love that God has set for us to follow. It's not emotion but self-sacrifice.

Now that is precisely what Paul is pointing out in 1 Corinthians 13. No matter what a person is like, how he behaves, or how he relates to you, you are to seek his highest good. That's what God did. And as God "sendeth rain on the just and on the unjust" (Matt. 5:45*b*), so you are to shower acts of self-sacrificing service on the deserving and the undeserving equally. Just remember, love is not an act of the emotion, it is an act of the will. To love somebody by an act of self-sacrifice is not a feeling. It is a determination that you make in your mind that this is right and this is what you will do.

2. The source of agape

You say, "John, how can I ever get to the place where I will be able to actually step out and touch the life of somebody—who is either deserving or undeserving, whom I care about or don't care about—and do an act of self-sacrificing service on his behalf? How can I ever get to that point?" Well, for one thing, you can't just whip it up. You can't get up in the morning and say, "Well, I've been cranky for three days, which is far too long, so today I will love everybody," then go look at your little poster that says, "Love never fails," then read a few Bible verses, and then go out and really love. No, you can't do that. It doesn't work that way at all.

You say, "Where does the capacity to love come from, then?" Well, when you walk in the Spirit (which means turning your

27

life over to His control, confessing your sin, and allowing the Spirit of God to govern your thought patterns), the Spirit of God will control you and produce fruit—one of which is love. Love will only come in that way. The way you are to approach it, then, is not in a self-righteous determination of your own mind; you are simply to yield your life to the Spirit of God, and the fruit of love will be manifest.

C. Love: Its Corruption in Corinth

The Corinthian church was not walking in the Spirit, yielded to the Spirit, or under the control of the Spirit. They were selfish, self-designing, self-willed, and self-motivated—doing everything they could to promote their own ends. It didn't matter what anybody else was doing or what anybody else needed—everybody was out for himself. In fact, that was the motto of the Corinthian church. They were not walking in the Spirit, so no love was produced. Everything they did manifested antagonism, rebellion, discord, disunity, and disharmony.

Now, it's precisely at this point that Paul speaks to the Corinthians in chapter 13 and says, "The only thing that's going to hang your whole assembly together is in love. The only way the spiritual gifts are going to operate is love. The only way you're going to stop the envy, jealousy, pride, and boasting that is present in your midst is to have love. Love is the key to the unity that will paint the portrait of Christ, so that the world can see what He really looks like."

Can unity exist without complete agreement?

If the people at Grace Church had to agree on everything to manifest unity and a single, visible testimony to the world, we'd be in a lot of trouble. Why? Because no matter what we do, somebody wouldn't agree with it. That's a fact. There is always someone who will say, "Well, I don't agree with the way that you're doing thus and so in such and such a place," or, "I don't agree with this certain situation," or, "I don't like where my class meets," or, "I don't agree with what the elders decided about this," or, "I wish they had put that pillar over there and that post over there," or, "Why aren't these things higher and why did they put the tree here?" There will always be people who disagree! I'll show you my mail. People disagree with me. In fact, when I finish preaching on Sundays, I hurry down the stairs before someone says something that will make me fall over. Once I'm down from the platform, I'm better able to handle their disgreements.

Not everybody agrees on everything in our church, but that isn't the point. We could never get everybody to agree on every little thing. However, what we want to do is this: We want everybody to love in a biblical way so that whether they agree or not is irrelevant. The priority is to sacrifice our own opinions for the sake of the unity of the whole. I don't always agree with every little thing that goes on in everybody's life, but sometimes I have to take a back seat and say, "I think the Lord is leading in a certain way, so I'm willing to lovingly acquiesce to somebody else." That's the spirit of unity.

Unity will never be on the basis of agreement, but agreement can be overruled by love. That's Paul's point in 1 Corinthians 13. The Corinthians had too many clashes going on. There was no way to get them all to think the same way, to agree on the same thing, or to have every little detail in the same box. That just wouldn't work. In fact, the only way that that can happen in a church is if the guy in the pulpit is an absolute dictator who drives out everybody who disagrees. But then you don't have a church—you have an absolute dictator with a whole bunch of rubber ducks quacking along behind him. That isn't true unity. True unity will come when all of the people, with all of their varying ideas and ideals, are willingly and lovingly anxious to sacrifice their own will for the sake of unity.

The Corinthians didn't even know the meaning of self-sacrifice. Everything they did was only for themselves. Can you imagine what it would be like to have everybody seeking the showy gifts, to have everybody trying to get the glory, and to have everybody trying to lead the group and be the spiritual big shots? Well, there was chaos—absolute chaos. So Paul stops in the middle of his discussion on spiritual gifts and says, "Now, let me talk to you about love. It doesn't matter what you do. It doesn't make any difference how many talents you have. It is irrelevant what your gifts are. It is inconsequential how seemingly great you are. Your popularity is absolutely unimportant. It doesn't matter how much power you have over other people. If you are not motivated and guided by the reality of self-sacrificing, caring, serving love, you are a spiritual zero. You're not even a one, you're a zero—you don't matter. You make no contribution if love is not the major contribution of your life."

Review

Now, what does Paul say specifically? In this chapter he discusses four aspects of love. He talks about the Prominence of Love, the Properties of Love, the Permanence of Love, and the Preeminence of Love. These four areas must be understood. In our last lesson we began to look at:

I. The Prominence of Love (vv. 1-3; see pp. 12-21)

"[If] I speak with the tongues of men and of angels, and have not love, I am become as sounding bronze, or a tinkling cymbal. And [if] I have the gift of prophecy, and understand all mysteries, and all knowledge; and [if] I have all faith, so that I could remove mountains, and have

29

not love, I am nothing. And [if] I bestow all my goods to feed the poor, and [if] I give my body to be burned, and have not love, it profiteth me nothing."

A. Languages Without Love Are Nothing (v. 1; see pp. 13-21)

We have already seen, in the Corinthian situation, that it didn't matter if someone had the gift of tongues or could even speak angel talk. It didn't matter—if there wasn't any love there. Being up front and speaking to crowds of people is a great experience. And eloquence is a characteristic that all speakers desire. People used to say that when Jonathan Edwards was done preaching the people would be lying on the ground, crying out to God for mercy. Imagine the power of that man's words! But even if you had that kind of eloquence and power in your speech, if you didn't have love, it wouldn't matter. To be able to convince people through speech, to capture their minds and their hearts, and to turn their wills to a certain behavior is a tremendous power. But it doesn't matter without love. To be able to play an audience like a master plays a piano—moving them to inspiration, to a calm, to an arousing, to a convincing, to a persuading, to a convicting—is an art that some men have mastered. But if they don't have love it doesn't matter. And in the case of the Corinthians, they had turned the gift of languages into a fleshly ecstasy—a fully pagan activity. So Paul said, "It doesn't matter, you've wasted it."

Now, that leads us into Paul's second point under his discussion of the prominence of love.

Love

B. Prophecy Without Love Is Nothing (v. 2a)

"And [if] I have the gift of prophecy . . . and have not love, I am nothing."

Prophecy without love is nothing. This goes further even than the gift of languages or speaking with the voice of angels. To have the gift of prophecy is to have the ultimate gift. In chapter 14, prophecy is hailed as the greatest of the gifts. Why? Because it is the proclamation of God's truth in the language that the people can hear and understand.

1. The elements of prophecy

I believe that prophecy has two aspects—revelation and reiteration. I want you to know that I speak the revelation of God—but not for the first time. I simply respeak it as I read it in the Bible. If you study, for example, the sermons of Peter, the sermons of Paul, and the sermon of Stephen, you will find that sometimes they were speaking new truth and sometimes they were quoting old truth—revelation and reiteration.

2. The expression of prophecy

If I had the ability to speak the Word of God for the first time or the power to proclaim old truth with force and meaning and dynamic and drama—without love it's nothing. Now the word "prophecy" means "to speak before someone." Paul is talking about those people who can stand up and publicly proclaim the truth of God eloquently and dramatically. The gift of prophecy is a tremendous gift. It includes the power to declare the things of God, the power to interpret life, the power to bring the Word of heaven to earth, the power to draw eternity into time. But without love, none of it matters. It is zero.

3. The enemies of prophecy

In Ephesians 4:15a Paul says, "But, speaking the truth in love." That's the balance to the gift of prophecy or preaching. I've always felt there are two great enemies of a preacher—a departure from the truth and a chilling indifference to the people. And, unfortunately, there are many preachers who are out of balance. There are some who have a great love for the people but don't ever diligently prepare so that they can give them the truth. And there are others who give out the truth, but could care less about the people. One has to fight to keep the balance.

Sometimes in my own ministry, just as I sit down to study, I'm presented with the fact that someone in my congregation has an immediate need that I should meet. I'm often caught in the balance between whether I should stop and go do a deed of self-sacrifice, or whether I should keep studying. Do I concentrate on preaching the truths of God (for which I have to study), or do I meet the needs of the people? That's not an easy question to answer, because preaching is also an act of love to the people. But that's the balance of priorities that all preachers must struggle with.

Unfortunately, there are many preachers who have opted out on both ends. In the name of love for people, some have watered down what they say to such an extent that they are not "speaking the truth" and giving those people the kind of love that will protect them from doctrinal error. On the other hand, there are pastors who decide to teach the truth of God without loving the people. Consequently, those people soon become convinced that God probably doesn't love them either. So there has to be a balance.

4. The examples of prophecy

a) Prophets without love

There are preachers (modern-day prophets) without love who have only one objective. That objective, according to Albert Barnes, a nineteenth-century minister and commentator, is not to feed the flock, but to fleece it. They don't love the people. They're only in the ministry for fame, power, prestige, personal gain, or to be somebody. They're up for the highest bidder. It's sad, but true.

Let me show you a biblical example of a prophet without love.

(1) Balaam

Numbers 24 gives us a good illustration of somebody who had the God-given gift of prophecy but didn't love the people. Consequently, he came out a zero. Let's begin at Numbers 24:15. "And he took up his parable, and said, Balaam, the son of Beor, hath said, and the man whose eyes are open hath said; he hath said, who heard the words of God, and knew the knowledge of the most High, who saw the vision of the Almighty, falling into a trance, but having his eyes open." Now there's a description of Balaam—a legitimate prophet who heard the words of God, knew the knowledge of the Most High, and saw the vision of the Almighty. This guy had the real gift.

Balaam's prophecy starts in verse 17, "I shall see him, but not now [something's coming, but not yet]: I shall behold him, but not near [it's going to be a while]: there shall come a Star out of Jacob, and a Scepter shall rise out of Israel." Who is he talking about? Well, the ultimate end of that prophecy is the Messiah (cf. Gen. 49:10). Here is a man with the gift of prophecy, who was given the marvelous, unequaled privilege of predicting the coming of the Messiah.

You say, "That's fantastic. Balaam must have really been something." No. He was nothing. Why? Look at verse 1 of chapter 25. At the end of the verse it says, "And the people began to commit harlotry with the daughters of Moab." Balaam had told the people about the Messiah, but the next thing we find out is that the people are committing harlotry with the daughters of Moab. You say, "Well, you sure can't blame that on Balaam. They probably just didn't listen to him."

Look at Numbers 31:16, and I'll show you why that isn't true. This is the commentary on Balaam's relationship to all the harlotry that was going on: "Behold, these [the Moabite women] caused the children of Israel, through the counsel of Balaam, to commit trespass against the Lord." You say, "Now wait a minute. Balaam? The prophet of God who knew the truth and spoke the truth?" It's the same guy, but the problem was, he didn't love the people. The Moabites came and said, "Hey, Balaam, how much do you want us to pay you to corrupt the people of Israel?" Well, they bought him off, and he enticed the children of Israel to commit whoredom with the Moabites. Look at the end of verse 8: "Balaam also, the son of Beor, they slew with the sword."

Throughout history we have recognized Balaam's ass as more acceptable in the ministry than Balaam, haven't we? Do you know why? Because he was a prophet who spoke the truth without loving the people. You see, genuine love and concern for the people is very important. In Balaam's case, it wasn't there. He prostituted love and turned it into hate. Consequently, the people entered into gross sin and Balaam lost his life.

(2) Counterfeit prophets

Matthew 7:21-23 gives another example of prophets without love—only these are counterfeit prophets. Jesus said, "Not every one that saith unto me, Lord, Lord, shall enter into the kingdom of heaven, but he that doeth the will of my Father, who is in heaven. Many will say to me in that day, Lord, Lord, have we not prophesied in thy name? . . . And them will I profess unto them, I never knew you; depart from me, ye that work iniquity." Counterfeit prophets.

To speak the truth without love is nothing—it's counterfeit—empty. And that applies to all the spiritual gifts. You may not have the gift of preaching, but you still have the same responsibility to exercise your gift with love. Do you really love the people you speak to about Christ? Do you do deeds of self-sacrifice for them? I believe that unless you do, you really haven't earned the right to speak the truth.

The Power of the Message Is the Motive

A young girl once came to me with tears in her eyes and said, "I teach a Sunday school class of little girls. I thought I loved them, but now I know that I really don't because I've never made any sacrifices on their behalf." Well, that's the essence of it. Do you love the people you preach to? Do you love the people you teach? Do you love them enough to make a sacrifice on their behalf in a personal way? You see, the power behind the message is the motive of the love of God in our hearts. The power of the message isn't vocabulary, cleverness, or diction. The power is the genuine, loving heart of the man or the woman who has the message. How much do you love?

Eloquence can be compared to a melodious organ or a screeching siren. Without love, eloquence is like a screeching siren, but with love it is like a melodious organ. The tongue, without love, is like a snake. It hisses and strikes and poisons with its venom. Only love gives the tongue gentleness and tenderness.

b) Prophets with love

(1) Jeremiah

Let me show you a prophet who *did* have love. His name is Jeremiah. He was a great fellow, but he had a hard ministry. Look at Jeremiah 1:5: "Before I formed thee in the womb, I knew thee; and before you camest forth out of the womb, I sanctified thee, and I ordained thee a prophet unto the nations." He didn't even have a choice, did he? People who struggle over the sovereignty of God should study the subject of God's call of the prophets. All of them were called the same way—Isaiah, Paul, Peter, and anybody else who proclaimed. Even the disciples were sovereignly called when Jesus walked along the beach and told them what to do. And so it was with Jeremiah.

Look at verses 6-7. "Then said I, Ah, Lord God! Behold, I cannot speak; for I am a child." In other words, "I've got a bad voice, my diction is lousy, and my mind isn't too sharp either. I'm rather infant in my understanding." "But the Lord said unto me, Say not, I am a child; for thou shalt go to all that I shall send thee, and whatsoever I command thee thou shalt speak." That sounds terrific, doesn't it? I wish the Lord had said that to me. No study or preparation—just go along, open your mouth, and God puts it in there. That would be great!

Well, by that time, Jeremiah was probably feeling pretty good about all that God had told him. Then verse 8 says, "Be not afraid of their face." What does that mean? Well, God was telling Jeremiah, "They're going to get ugly when you talk, and they're going to screw up their faces and be very upset at you. But don't be afraid of it." Why? "For I am with thee to deliver thee, saith the Lord."

Now look at verses 9-10. "Then the Lord put forth his hand, and touched my mouth. And the Lord said unto me, Behold, I have put my words in thy mouth. See, I have this day set thee over the nations and over the kingdoms, to root out, and to pull down, and to destroy, and to throw down, to build, and to plant." Now, that's probably the greatest verse in the Bible on the power of preaching. Preaching is the ability to rule nations and kingdoms, to root out, pull down, destroy, throw down, build, and plant. There is tremendous power in preaching, and God told Jeremiah, "You're going to have that power."

Continuing on in verses 16-18*a*, God says, "And I will

utter my judgments against them touching all their wickedness. . . . Thou, therefore, gird up thy loins, and arise, and speak unto them all that I command thee; be not dismayed at their faces, lest I confound thee before them." In other words, "If you start doubting and getting afraid, I'll make you look bad." "For, behold, I have made thee this day a fortified city, and an iron pillar, and bronze walls against the whole land." By now Jeremiah was probably saying, "I'm going to give it to them and stick my ground. I'm going to be an iron pillar—very insensitive. I don't care what they say!"

Here's Jeremiah—an iron pillar, a bronze wall, a fortified city. In chapter 4, however, you'll see this prophet's spirit. He's been in the ministry for a while, and he's starting to get a little feedback from the people. Look at his attitude in verse 19. "My distress, my distress! I am pained at my very heart; my heart maketh a noise in me; I cannot hold my peace, because thou hast heard, O my soul, the sound of the trumpet, the alarm of war." He's saying to these people, "You're going to get taken into captivity and you're going to be destroyed. A war is coming, the Babylonians are coming, and I can't stand it—it makes my heart run and my soul grieve." You see, Jeremiah loved his people—he cared.

Look at chapter 8, verse 18. Jeremiah says, "When I would comfort myself against sorrow, my heart is faint in me." He feels like he's going to have a heart attack. That's how much anxiety he has. Why? Because of "the voice of the cry of the daughter of my people" (v. 19a). Further, in 9:1 he says, "Oh, that my head were waters, and mine eyes a fountain of tears, that I might weep day and night for the slain of the daughter of my people!"

Jeremiah was a man with a broken heart, a man with tears, a man who cared, a man who loved. And you can go right on through the book of Jeremiah and find incident after incident of Jeremiah's tears. He's the weeping prophet.

(2) Paul

The apostle Paul was a man who did a lot of weeping too. In Acts 20:19, he says that he served the Lord "with many tears." In Romans 9:2-3, he weeps over Israel. In 2 Corinthians 2:4, he weeps over the carnal Christians. In Acts 20:31, he weeps over the influence of false teachers. He cried his way through his ministry because he cared.

Paul and Jeremiah had the balance between love and truth—Balaam didn't. To exercise the gift of prophecy apart from deep love for God, deep love for His Word, and deep love for His people and to do it for self-glory, fame, success, pride, or from indifference, is to be a zero in God's eyes—no matter what you are in the eyes of the world.

Languages without love are nothing, prophecy without love is nothing, and third:

C. Knowledge Without Love Is Nothing (v. 2b)

"And [if] I . . . understand all mysteries, and all knowledge . . . and have not love, I am nothing."

1. The specifics of knowledge

   a) "All mysteries"

   What does it mean to "understand all mysteries"? Well, first let's define the term "mysteries." This term, which is used over thirty times in Scripture, is always used in a technical way to refer to a divine truth revealed in the New Testament. In other words, a mystery in the Bible is "something hidden in the past which is now revealed." Some of these New Testament mysteries, for example, are:

   (1) The mystery of God in human flesh (Col. 2:2-3, 9; 1 Tim. 3:16)

   (2) The mystery of Christ in us (Col. 1:26-27)

   (3) The mystery of the church as a body (Eph. 3:3-6, 9)

   (4) The mystery of iniquity (2 Thess. 2:7)

   There are many things in the New Testament that are referred to as mysteries—something that was hidden and now is revealed. And we are the ones who know these sacred secrets of God. In Matthew 13:11, Jesus calls these secrets "mysteries of the kingdom of heaven." And according to Matthew 11:25, He said that these things were "hidden . . . from the wise and prudent, and . . . revealed . . . unto babes." Furthermore, a mystery is a sacred secret that is related to God's redemptive plan and His ultimate plan for history.

   So God has certain redemptive truths that He has revealed to us. But there are others that He hasn't revealed. Let's assume, though, that you knew every redemptive fact and could perfectly correlate every redemptive truth. Let's also assume that you knew every single fact about God's ultimate purpose for time and eternity and could correlate all of those facts. If you knew all of that and didn't have love, you would still be nothing.

   b) "All knowledge"

   What does it mean to have "all knowledge"? The Greek word here for knowledge is *gnōsis* and refers to facts that can be ascertained by investigation.

So let's say that you knew every secret relative to redemption and God's plan for the ages and every single fact in existence in the universe. If you knew all of that and didn't have love, how would you rate on a scale of one to five? "Well," you say, "I'd be at least a two or a three." No, you'd be zero. You wouldn't even be a one. Why? Because love is important. Of course, you can't know all of those things. That's why Paul uses the Greek word *ean* with the subjunctive case. It's all hypothetical. But even if you could understand all mysteries and have all knowledge, without love you'd be a zero.

2. The superiority of love

It always amazes me that there are some people who think that because they know everything, they have no responsibility to love anybody. There are people who have all their doctrine systematized and categorized and have all the theological answers. But if they don't have love, do you know what they are in God's eyes? They're nothings—big zeros. Why? Because love is superior to intellectual eminence.

Have you ever heard of anyone with a Ph.D. in love? People receive the title doctor for their intellectual eminence. Our value system isn't all it ought to be, is it? Spiritual insight into the Scriptures is nothing but spiritual snobbery, Pharisaism, and condescension if there is no love. You see, knowledge without love kills, but with love, knowledge gives life. Knowledge without love is ugly, but with love, knowledge is beautiful. Knowledge without love is impotent, but with love, knowledge is powerful.

In 1 Corinthians 8:1*b*, Paul hints at this when he says, "Knowledge puffeth up, but love edifieth [builds up]." If you have a choice between learning to love and learning some fact, learn to love. The Bible emphasizes this again and again. Now, knowledge is important. God doesn't want a whole bunch of loving ignoramuses who will love themselves right into all kinds of error. He doesn't want us to "love" so much that we won't make any discrimination between who's right and who's wrong, who's saved and who's not. We must have knowledge, but it must be combined with love.

In Philippians 1:9, Paul says, "And this I pray, that your love may abound yet more and more in knowledge." Do you see? You can't separate love and knowledge. They must be kept in perfect balance. However, if you have a choice between going to a class or worship service to learn something, or stopping to help someone on your way who just had a flat tire, stop and fix the flat tire. Love is better than knowledge.

D. Faith Without Love Is Nothing (v. 2*c*)

"And [if] I have all faith, so that I could remove mountains, and have not love, I am nothing."

1. **The gift of faith discussed**

The concept of faith can take many, many directions. But here in 1 Corinthians 13:2, Paul is talking about the gift of faith, not saving faith. He's referring to the kind of faith expressed in prayer that releases God's power.

a) Matthew 17:20

In Matthew 17:20, Jesus responds to the disciples' question regarding why they couldn't cast a demon out of a child. He says, "Because of your unbelief; for verily I say unto you, If ye have faith as a grain of mustard seed, ye shall say unto this mountain, Move from here to yonder place; and it shall move; and nothing shall be impossible unto you." In other words, Jesus was saying, "If you have the faith to believe God in prayer, you can move mountains." Now, a lot of people get confused by this verse and say, "I've never seen anyone do that." Well, that isn't the point. God doesn't want people literally moving mountains. That would cause all kinds of problems, wouldn't it? Jesus is not speaking of moving mountains in a literal sense.

b) Matthew 21:21

In Matthew 21:21, Jesus says to His disciples, "If ye have faith, and doubt not, ye shall . . . say unto this mountain [the Mount of Olives], Be thou removed, and be thou cast into the sea, it shall be done." Now Jesus doesn't want the Mount of Olives dumped into the Dead Sea. That would mess up the Second Coming. That isn't His point. He is simply talking about people who have the gift of faith.

2. **The gift of faith defined**

The gift of faith is the ability to believe God continually. It is trusting God when everyone else is questioning Him. It is seen in the person who stands firm and says, "God is still on the throne. So I'm just asking Him to accomplish His purpose, and waiting for Him to release His power." The person with the gift of faith goes through every trial like a rock while the rest of us are falling apart. That person is able to wait confidently in God until His power is released and he begins to see why God did what He did. Those who have the gift of faith pray and pray with the kind of trust in God that never gives up. And it's that kind of faith that can remove mountains.

Now the mountains that faith can remove are not literal mountains. In Matthew 16, Jesus starts talking in parables. So when He talks about a mountain in chapter 17, there is contextual precedence that He's referring to a mountain in terms of an analogy. He doesn't want people moving mountains around; that would be ridiculous. That doesn't accomplish anything. Further, Zechariah 4:6b-7a says, "Not by might, nor by power, but by my Spirit, saith the Lord of hosts. Who art thou, O great mountain?" Now, he's not talking about an actual mountain. He's saying, "When I have the power of God, what mountain can stand in front of that?" So the gift of faith is the ability to believe God to do things that most people wouldn't hold still to see happen.

What Paul is saying is this: "If you had all faith, faith that never doubted God or even had a tinge of question; if you were such a rock that nothing was impossible for you to believe, nothing brought a question to your mind, nothing was a cause for doubt; if you never shook, never wavered in anything, and never questioned God—without love you'd be a nothing." That's incredible. Paul is knocking the pins out from under everybody. It doesn't matter what gifts you have, how eloquent you are, what you know, or what you believe. You could be a celebrated Christian, theologian, missionary, pastor, teacher, author, or scholar. But if you don't have the agape of God as the driving force of your life, you're a nothing. It's that simple. So check your motive.

E. Benevolence Without Love Is Nothing (v. 3*a*)

"And [if] I bestow all my goods to feed the poor . . . and have not love, it profiteth me nothing."

Love is self-sacrifice, but all self-sacrifice is not necessarily love. Did you get that? There are a lot of people living sacrificially and doing a lot of strange things for a religion they believe in. However, they're not doing it out of love; they're doing it out of fear and self-righteousness. You can do self-sacrificial deeds for many different reasons. Paul says, "Love is self-sacrifice, but self-sacrifice is not necessarily love. So make sure your motive is love."

1. The meaning specified

The word "feed," in verse 3, is from the Greek verb *psomizō.* The noun form of this word, *psomion,* means "morsel." Here is someone who is literally giving away his fortune one morsel at a time. In other words, his giving is the ultimate act of benevolence. He's not just writing a check for the fund to feed the poor, he is going out and giving every little morsel away—piece by piece. So if I was involved in the actual act of charity—personally giving each small gift to large numbers of individual people—it wouldn't matter if I didn't have love. If I did it for obligation's sake, if I did it out of legalism, if I did it to salve my conscience, if I did it to get recognition (like Ananias and Sapphira), if I did it because of peer pressure, it would mean nothing.

2. The motive scrutinized

a) The improper motives

When you go to church and give money to the Lord, why do

you give? Do you feel obligated to give? Do you feel you have to give to earn God's favor? Do you give to pacify your conscience for a sinful week, hoping God will balance the scale? Do you give to get recognition from the people around you? Do you tell people what you give? Do you feel peer pressure that if you don't give, you won't be able to talk about it the next time the group gets together? Well, if you give for any of those reasons, you're a zero.

b) The proper motive

What's the only proper motive for giving? Love! That's why we're to do it secretly—privately. It doesn't matter how benevolent you are if you don't love. Luke 18:11-12 says, "The Pharisee stood and prayed thus with himself, God, I thank thee that I am not as other men are, extortioners, unjust, adulterers, or even as this publican. I fast twice in the week; I give tithes of all that I possess." Well, Jesus said, "This Pharisee is a zero!" However, the publican "went down to his house justified rather than the other" (v. 14*a*). Benevolence without love is nothing.

F. Martyrdom Without Love Is Nothing (v. 3*b*)

"And [if] I give my body to be burned, and have not love, it profiteth me nothing."

1. The possible interpretations

There are different interpretations about what Paul was referring to by the phrase "give my body to be burned." For example:

a) Branded to become a slave

Some think it means to become a slave. In those days when a person became a slave, they branded him with a hot iron that burned his flesh. Some say that Paul is saying, "Even if I become a slave, it wouldn't matter." That's a possible interpretation.

b) Burned to become a martyr

In line with the ultimate nature of Paul's discussion in 1 Corinthians 13, it would seem to me that he might be saying something like this: "Even if I gave my life to be burned at the stake, it wouldn't matter." Now the argument against this interpretation is, "Well, there was no precedent for burning people at the stake. That didn't go on in Paul's day." Well, that's true. There was not a burning-at-the-stake persecution at the time of Paul. Christians were burned at the stake at a later date. There are, however, several ways to look at it.

(1) Future Persecution

Paul could have been referring to the burning that was

going to come. And he also could have been looking forward to those many Christians who were going to die at the stake for the wrong reasons. One of the interesting things about the martyrdom of the early church is that many Christians of that time developed a martyr complex—wanting to die as martyrs in order to become famous like other Christians who had died as martyrs. It's possible that Paul was anticipating that situation by virtue of the insight of the Holy Spirit.

(2) Past persecution

There's another possibility too. There were some men in the past who gave their lives to be burned. Shadrach, Meshach and Abednego, though God delivered them, were willing to be burned (Dan. 3:16-18).

(3) Local illustration

The following story is another possibility. In the city of Athens, which was near Corinth, there was a tomb called "the Indian's tomb." A certain Indian, on that very spot, had set himself on fire and burned himself to death. Prior to his suicide, however, he had written the following epitaph: "Zamanochegas, an Indian from Bargosa, according to the traditional customs of the Indians, made himself immortal and lies here." Here was a man who burned his body to gain some religious immortality. Maybe Paul had that in mind.

2. The personal motive

Whether Paul was referring to the ultimate act of becoming a slave or to the ultimate act of burning at the stake and dying as a martyr, without love it doesn't matter. A Christian martyr in the second century, a kamikaze, a Buddhist who burns himself, or a missionary eaten by cannibals—none of it matters if the motive is not love. And I don't think it's cynical to recall that many early Christians sought to be burned so that they could remain famous as martyrs. I also don't think it's cynical to say that deeds that look sacrificial on the surface are usually the products of pride.

The sum of it is this: Languages, or prophecy, or knowledge, or benevolence, or martyrdom don't mean anything without love. It didn't matter what the Corinthians did, if they did it without love. And it doesn't matter what you do, if you do it without love. If the motive isn't love, it adds up to nothing. In fact, you can look at this passage in the following way: Verse 1 says, "The loveless person produces nothing of value." Verse 2 says, "The loveless person is himself of no value." Verse 3 says, "The loveless person receives nothing of value." Life minus love equals zero.

Revelation 2:2-4 says this to the church at Ephesus, "I know thy works, and thy labor, and thy patience, and how thou canst not bear them who are evil; and thou hast tried them who say they are apostles, and are not, and hast found them liars; and hast borne, and hast patience, and for my name's sake hast labored, and hast not fainted." They had worked hard and they had right doctrine. "Nevertheless, I have somewhat against thee, because thou hast left thy first love." Do you know what the Lord did? He removed the candlestick, the church died, and it's never been there since. Any church can be in the same situation if it doesn't have love—and so can you as a person.

Focusing on the Facts

1. In our English language, the word *love* has many different meanings. Is this true in the Greek language? Explain (see p. 26)?

2. What is the Greek word for love in 1 Corinthians 13? What is the definition of that word (see p. 26)?

3. What insight into the meaning of love does Jesus give us in Matthew 5:44 (see p. 27)?

4. Is biblical love an emotion? Explain (see p. 27).

5. How is it possible for us to love others in the same way that God loves us (see pp. 27-28)?

6. Can unity exist without complete agreement? What is the key to unity (see pp. 28-29)?

7. According to 1 Corinthians 14, what is the greatest spiritual gift (see p. 29)?

8. What are the two elements of the gift of prophecy (see p. 30)?

9. Define the gift of prophecy (see p. 31).

10. What are the two great enemies that a preacher must watch out for as he exercises his gift of prophecy (see p. 31)?

11. What verse succinctly describes the balance that must go along with the gift of prophecy? What happens to a man's ministry if this balance is not maintained (see p. 31)?

12. Was Balaam a legitimate, God-ordained prophet? Support your answer. What caused the downfall of his ministry (see pp. 32-33)?

13. The prophet Jeremiah is an example of a prophet who _____ love. This is evidenced by his nickname, "the _____ prophet" (see pp. 34-35).

14. The apostle Paul served the Lord "with many tears" (Acts 20:19). What were some of the things that caused him to weep (see p. 35)?

15. What is a "mystery" in the New Testament? Give some examples (see p. 36).

16. What areas of truth do "mysteries" deal with (see p. 36)?

17. How does the term "knowledge" differ from the term "mysteries" in 1 Corinthians 13:2 (see p. 37)?

18. Is it possible for us to "understand all mysteries, and all knowledge"? Support your answer (see p. 37).

19. What does knowledge without love accomplish? What happens when people have love without knowledge? What does Philippians 1:9 say about love and knowledge? Of the two, which is superior (see p. 37)?

20. What is the gift of faith? Explain the concept of faith's moving mountains (see p. 38)?

21. Love is self-sacrifice, but is all self-sacrifice love? Explain (see p. 39).

22. What light is shed on the meaning of 1 Corinthians 13:3a by understanding the meaning of the Greek word for "feed" (see p. 39)?

23. What are some of the improper motives behind many of the benevolent acts that people are involved in? What is the only proper motive (see p. 40)?

24. What are the possible interpretations of the phrase "give my body to be burned" in 1 Corinthians 13:3b? Which one is most likely the best? Why (see pp. 40-41)?

25. What's the best way to sum up 1 Corinthians 13:1-3 (see p. 41)?

26. Fill in the following equation: Life − Love = _____ (see p. 41).

27. According to Revelation 2:2-4, what was praiseworthy about the church at Ephesus? However, what was their downfall (see p. 42)?

Pondering the Principles

1. What did Jesus mean when He told us to love our enemies (Matthew 5:44)? How is that possible? Why are we to love our enemies, according to verse 45? Can you think of someone you would consider your enemy? Take a moment and consider how you can do good to him through an act of self-sacrificial service. Then commit yourself to do it, making sure your motive is love and your power is the Spirit of God.

2. Is complete agreement necessary for unity in the Body of Christ? What is the key to unity? Is there a particular brother or sister in Christ whom you find yourself always disagreeing with or always disagreeing with you? If so, memorize and meditate on Philippians 2:3-4 and ask God to show you how to love him or her in practical ways.

3. If you teach—whether it be a Sunday school class, a home Bible study, or a one-on-one discipleship group—ask yourself the following questions: Do you love those that you teach? When was the last time you made a sacrifice on their behalf? What was it? How does God view your teaching if it is not motivated by love? Spend some time with the Lord in prayer to determine your real motive for teaching. If it isn't love, confess it to God, examine your heart for any other unconfessed sin and confess it to God, and then allow the Holy Spirit to enable you to exercise your spiritual gift with His love.

4. Read the following verses: Hosea 4:6, Romans 12:2, 1 Corinthians 1:5; Ephesians 1:17-18, Colossians 1:9, 2 Peter 1:5; 3:18. Is knowledge important in the life of a Christian? Why? According to 1 Corinthians 8:1, what can knowledge produce? What will prevent this from happening (see Phil. 1:9)? According to 1 Corinthians 8:1 and 13:2, what is superior to knowledge? With all of that in mind, what should you do if you're on your way to a Bible study and you see someone who needs help changing a flat tire or someone who needs help pushing a car that's out of gas? Once you've determined what you *should* do, is that what you *would* do? Read Revelation 2:2-4 and evaluate whether or not you're like the Ephesian church, which had knowledge and good works without love. Now commit yourself to live a life of love—a life of self-sacrificial service in the power of God.

5. Explain the following statement: Love is self-sacrifice, but all self-sacrifice is not necessarily love. Have you ever given to the poor and needy or even given to the church with one of the following reasons: a sense of obligation, peer pressure, legalism, to pacify a guilty conscience, to get recognition, to earn God's favor? What is the only proper motive for giving? What does God think of your sacrificial act or your gift if your motives are wrong? What are some practical ways to keep your motives pure when you give to the Lord or to others?

3
The Qualities of True Love—
Part 1

Outline

Introduction
A. Love's Adulation
B. Love's Absence
C. Love's Activity

Review
I. The Prominence of Love

Lesson
II. The Perfections (Properties) of Love
   A. Love Is Patient
      1. The meaning of patience
         a) Its uniqueness to Christianity
         b) Its usage in the New Testament
      2. The models of patience
         a) God
            (1) Romans 2:4
            (2) 2 Peter 3:9
         b) Jesus Christ
         c) Stephen
   B. Love Is Kind
      1. The meaning of kindness
         a) Compared with patience
         b) Clarified by the Greek
      2. The models of kindness
         a) God
            (1) Romans 2:4
            (2) Titus 3:4
            (3) 1 Peter 2:3
         b) Jesus Christ
   C. Love Is Not Jealous
      1. Jealousy dichotomized
         a) Superficial jealousy
         b) Deep-rooted jealousy

2. Jealousy discussed
3. Jealousy displayed
4. Jealousy disarmed
5. Jealousy documented
    a) Eve
    b) Cain
    c) Joseph's brothers
    d) The prodigal son's brother
6. Jealousy denounced
    a) Proverbs 27:4
    b) James 3:14-16
7. Jealousy defeated

Introduction

A. Love's Adulation

The greatest commodity in the world—the *summum bonum* of life—is love. First Corinthians 13:13*b* says, "The greatest of these is love." First Peter 4:8*a* says, "And above all things have fervent love." And when the Bible wants to define God it says, "God is love" (1 John 4:8*b*). Love is the clearest definition of God—the personification of His character. Romans 13:10*b* says, "Love is the fulfilling of the law." Love is the high point of everything—the number one ingredient necessary to attune one's life to the character of God.

B. Love's Absence

It's sad to say that love—as urgent, as important, and as divine as it is—is very frequently missing from God's own people, the church. One great illustration of that is the church in the city of Corinth—a church in which existed the multiplicity of spiritual gifts, a wealth of human teachers ranging all the way from the apostle Paul to Apollos, the finest of teaching, a great grasp on doctrine, and a great facility for reaching the lost in a strategic city. But even with all that going for them, Paul said it added up to zero. Why? Because love was missing—and anything minus love equals zero. So in 1 Corinthians 13, the apostle Paul points out the absolute necessity and urgency of love—love that was tragically absent in their community of believers. And strangely enough, even as important as it is, it's still very difficult for the church to truly experience love.

C. Love's Activity

The word that is used throughout 1 Corinthians 13 for "love" is the Greek word *agapē*—the strongest, the most grandiose, the loftiest, the most fully defining word to speak of this particular characteristic. There have been many definitions, many books, many songs, many poems, and many discussions about love. But when you've said it all, and you've read it all, and you've sung it all, and you've heard it all, you haven't even scratched the surface until you've looked at 1 Corinthians 13:4-7. These verses contain the most complete description of love ever penned. I say that because this is God's own personal definition of love.

Frankly, if you want to be technical, the Bible never defines love. It never defines love in terms of abstracts, attitudes, feelings, or ideologies; it only describes love. And it only describes love in terms of action. Why? Because love is not an abstract, it is not a feeling, it is not an attitude; love is a deed—an activity. To support this, I want to point out something to you that you wouldn't know unless you were aware of the Greek. When you look at verses 4 to 7 in the English, it says: "Love is patient, love is kind, love is this, love is not that, and so forth." In the English, love is described with adjectives. But in the Greek, each of these descriptions of love is a verb—and verbs describe action. So, love is not something you describe with adjectives; love is something you describe with verbs. Love is only love when it acts.

The Corinthians had desperately missed the boat, because in all of their activity there was no love. So Paul, in the midst of his discussion about spiritual gifts, stops in chapter 13 to talk to them about love. Chapter 13 breaks down into four points: the Prominence of Love (vv. 1-3), the Perfections (or Properties) of Love (vv. 4-7), the Permanence of Love (vv. 8-12), and the Preeminence of Love (v. 13).

Review

I. The Prominence of Love (vv. 1-3; see pp. 12-21, 29-42)

Paul wanted the Corinthians to understand that love is a necessary reality and that without it they were nothing. Pointing out the prominence of love in verses 1-3, he says, "It doesn't matter whether you can speak in tongues—even the tongues of angels. You're nothing but noise if you don't have love. It doesn't matter if you have the gift of prophecy; it doesn't matter if you have all knowledge, all wisdom, and all faith; and it doesn't even matter if you die as a martyr, or sell everything you have and give it to the poor. If you don't have love, you're nothing—absolutely nothing." Love plays the prominent part in all Christian behavior. And where it is absent, the behavior ceases to be Christian.

Lesson

II. The Perfections (Properties) of Love (vv. 4-7)

"Love suffereth long, and is kind; love envieth not; love vaunteth not itself, is not puffed up, doth not behave itself unseemly, seeketh not its own, is not easily provoked, thinketh no evil, rejoiceth not in iniquity, but rejoiceth in the truth; beareth all things, believeth all things, hopeth all things, endureth all things."

47

That's Paul's description of love. You didn't see anything abstract or ideological, did you? The entire description is in terms of behavior. In fact, Paul's description of love could be compared to what happens when a beam of light hits a prism. As the prism divides a single beam of light into all of its colors, so the apostle Paul takes the concept of love, shoots it into the prism, and comes out with fifteen different colors—all of which describe the perfections that make up the one reality of love. First Corinthians 13:4-7 is the spectrum of love—love in action.

How do you match up?

The descriptions of love in 1 Corinthians 13 are not things you don't understand. They're simply things you and I don't apply. My approach in this passage is not to just tell you what it says—you can read it for yourself—but to try to help you to see how to apply it. Now, it isn't important that you evaluate my methods and say, "Well, his first subpoint is not very strong, and I don't get point two. He seems to be a little disorganized. That isn't a very good illustration—it doesn't apply," and so on. It isn't important that you get analytical. It isn't even important that you say, "Boy, that was terrific! I really liked that!" What is important is that you put your life up against the characteristics of love and see how you come out. That's what matters! Nothing else is important.

The apostle Paul doesn't list the fifteen perfections of love in any logical order, but he could be listing them in the order of their abuse in the Corinthian church. He starts out, for example, by saying, "Love suffereth long," which is just like a slap in the face to the Corinthians, who were totally impatient and intolerant. Then he says, "Love . . . is kind," which they were far from fulfilling. And when he said, "Love envieth not," their jealousy and envy was exposed. According to the entire first part of the third chapter, they were definitely jealous and envious.

You see, Paul is showing them, openly and honestly, where they fall short in the area of love. He's saying to them, "Here is love and here you are—check it out. Realize that nothing you do matters because of your lack of love. And just so you'll know why I say that, I'll describe love so that you can see where you are having your problems." We, too, can match up our lives to these fifteen perfections of love and see where we fall short.

Let me add this—I believe that when Paul was painting this portrait of love, Jesus was his model. This passage describes Him. Every one of these principles could be taken back into the gospels and compared to Christ's life, and you would see that each one is true of Him. But that's to be expected, because 1 Corinthians 13 is how God describes

48

love, and God is love and Christ is God.

Let's look at the first one.

A. Love Is Patient (v. 4a)

"Love suffereth long."

1. The meaning of patience

Love is patient (Gk., *makrothumeō* [vb.] or *makrothumia* [n.]). This word is used again and again in the New Testament to describe patience with people. It isn't a word that concerns itself with circumstances or events; it concerns itself with people. It is the ability to be wronged and wronged again and have the power to retaliate but never even think of it. Chrysostom, the early church Father, said, "It is the word which is used of the man who is wronged and who has it easily in his power to avenge himself but will never do it." That's the word. It is the spirit that never retaliates. It describes the person who never ever gets angry.

a) Its uniqueness to Christianity

Did you know that patience with people was strictly a Christian concept? You say, "What do you mean by that?" Well, in the Greek world, this was never considered to be a virtue; it was considered to be a sign of weakness. In fact, Aristotle defined the great Greek virtue as the refusal to tolerate any insult or injury and a readiness to strike back at any hurt. That was a virtue. According to the Greeks, you were a big man if you really whacked away at your enemies. If you retaliated and were full of vengeance, you were showing your strength. You were never to let anyone get away with anything.

We can identify with that, can't we? We make heroes out of people who strike back, and say, "Boy, there's a gutsy guy. He sure told him off." We think that's courageous. We think a man is someone who will defend himself if insulted and verbally assail any offender. That's heroism to us, but to God it's the very opposite of love. Love does not retaliate. Now this was something new to the Greeks, but Christians were to be characterized by love.

b) Its usage in the New Testament

The word *makrothumeō* literally means "to be long tempered." It describes someone with a long fuse. This word appears many times throughout the New Testament. Paul said it was characteristic of his own heart (2 Cor. 6:6) and that it should be characteristic of every Christian (Eph. 4:2). In fact, it is one of the fruit of the Spirit (Gal. 5:22).

2. The models of patience

Now, if you need a model to follow, it's not too hard to find some.

a) God

(1) Romans 2:4—The person who rejects God's grace is really despising "the riches of his goodness and forbearance and long-suffering." Somebody who constantly turns his back on God is despising God's patience—His long-suffering.

(2) 2 Peter 3:9—God "is long-suffering—not willing that any should perish."

So one model to follow, in terms of patience, is God. You say, "Well, it's kind of hard to model my life after God. He's too abstract." Then how about Christ?

b) Jesus Christ

While the Lord Jesus Christ was hanging on the cross, after He had endured all that He had endured, He said this about His killers: "Father, forgive them; for they know not what they do" (Luke 23:34*a*).

You say, "Jesus is hard for me to model after, too." Well, how would you like to try Stephen? He's a little more earthy.

c) Stephen

As he was dying under the crushing blows of their stones, Stephen said, "Lord, lay not this sin to their charge" (Acts 7:60). He was long tempered—no vengeance, no retaliation, no bitterness, no animosity, no fighting back.

Can you imagine what the church would be like if nobody ever sought revenge? Can you imagine what your home would be like if everyone had a long fuse? Men, after your wife has done something you didn't like, have you ever found yourself silently saying, "I'll show her! See if she gets another word out of me. See if she gets that new dress. I'll come home late from work and the dinner will be cold. That'll really get her!"? Well, that's the spirit of retaliation, but it isn't love, is it? Love can be wronged and wronged and wronged without ever wanting revenge. That's the way to define love.

The Patience of the Eternal God

Robert Ingersoll, the brilliant atheist of the last century (if any atheist could be classified as brilliant), stopped in the middle of one of his lectures against God, took out his watch, held it up to his audience, and made the following challenge: "I'll give God five minutes to strike me dead for the things I've said." Well, he wasn't struck dead, so he just continued to mock God. Somebody related this incident to the great Christian Theodore Parker, who smiled and said, "And did the gentleman think he could exhaust the patience of the eternal God in five minutes?"

God is patient, isn't He? Aren't you glad? If He wasn't, we would all have been wiped out a long time ago. I've heard people say, "Oh, but how can I be patient? I've been wronged again and again." That may be true, but God could say that about you, couldn't He? Think about the story of Israel—the record of a patient love on the part of God for a rebellious, disobedient, sinful, disloyal people. You say, "Yeah, they were really horrible!" Well, before you say that too loud, it sounds a lot like our biographies too. If God was impatient, we'd all be long gone. But God is a long-suffering God—a powerful feature of love.

The Effect Patience Has on Hate

When you deal with people, patience (a lack of retaliation) has a tremendous effect. A great example of this is shown in a story about Abraham Lincoln. Abraham Lincoln made a lot of friends, but he also made some enemies. One of his most outspoken enemies was a man named Stanton. Stanton just despised Lincoln. In fact, in print he called him "a low, cunning clown." On one occasion, he nicknamed him "the original gorilla" and said that it was ridiculous for people to go to Africa to find a gorilla, when they could easily find one in Springfield, Illinois. He was very bitter toward Lincoln, but Lincoln never replied to any of Stanton's attacks. He never said a word to him. However, when it came time to choose a war minister for the United States government, Lincoln chose Stanton. When asked why he chose someone who had opposed him so vehemently, Lincoln replied, "Because he's the best man for the job."

The years wore on until that fateful day of Lincoln's assassination. His biographer writes, "The night when the assassin's bullet tore out Lincoln's life, in the little room to which the President's body was taken, there stood that same Stanton. Looking down into the silent face of Lincoln in all its ruggedness, he spoke the following words through his tears: 'There lies the greatest ruler of men the world has ever seen.' " He never accepted Lincoln's politics, but he couldn't resist the non-retaliating spirit of the man. Love forgives seventy times seven when it's been wronged.

This leads us to the second attribute:

B. Love Is Kind (v. 4b)

"Love . . . is kind."

1. The meaning of kindness

   a) Compared with patience

   Kindness is the flip side of patience. Long-suffering endures

51

the injuries of others, and kindness pays them back with good deeds. Long-suffering says, "I'll *take* anything from my enemies," but kindness says, "I'll *give* anything to my enemies to meet their need." That's the essence of kindness. It's just the other side of long-suffering.

b) Clarified by the Greek

In the Greek, the root word for kindness means "useful." So Paul is saying, "I will do anything that will be of use to another—even my enemy. I will live my life to benefit others." That's what Paul means when he says that love is kind. It's useful to other people. Love is not an abstract concept; it's a deed of kindness, a deed of generosity, an act that you do for someone who has a need. The kindness Paul is talking about isn't the sweet attitude that we often connect with the word; it's the idea of being useful to others. When Jesus said, "Love your enemies" (Matt. 5:44*a*), He didn't say, "Feel good about them." However, in that same verse, He did say, "Do good to them."

Incidentally, Paul is not describing love in ideal surroundings, by any means. He's not talking to a group of people who have a warm affection for each other and wonderful friendships. These people in the Corinthian church are at each other's throats. So Paul says, "In the hard surroundings of a sinful, selfish church, and in the hard environment of an evil world that brings negative influences to bear on love, that's the atmosphere in which the true character of love will really shine."

2. The models of kindness

Now, who are the models of kindness—love that does good things for others?

a) God

   (1) Romans 2:4—Paul said, "Or despisest thou the riches of his goodness . . . not knowing that the goodness of God leadeth thee to repentance?" God repeatedly does things to benefit even His enemies, does He not?

   (2) Titus 3:4—Paul wrote, "But after the kindness and love of God, our Savior, toward man appeared." God performs deeds of kindness.

   (3) 1 Peter 2:3—"If so be ye have tasted that the Lord is gracious." The word "gracious" is the same Greek word that is translated "kind." God is kind. He does good, useful, helpful things for people.

b) Jesus Christ

In Matthew 11:29-30, Jesus says, "Take my yoke upon you, and learn of me. . . . For my yoke is easy, and my burden is light." The word "easy," in the Greek, is the same word that is translated "kind" in 1 Corinthians 13. Jesus is simply saying, "Join up with Me and I'll express My kindness to you." It's a tremendous thought.

Kindness can heal the hurts of the world, as well as the hurts in your family. Let me ask you, married people, are you kind to each other? Is your first thought, "What can I do that would be useful, helpful, and meaningful to my partner?" just after you've been irritated or hurt? Do you say to yourself, "How can I repay his anger with kindness?" or, "How can I repay his hurt with something useful and good that he needs to have done?"?

Let me ask you, parents, are you kind to your children? Do they sense a tenderness in you? Do you go out of your way to do kind things for them, or do you try to buy them off because of your lack of kindness? Do you go the second mile with them, or would you rather not be bothered? Are you willing to make some sacrifices to be helpful to them? Now that gets real practical in our house. "Dad," my son says to me, "would you help me study for my test?" Well, that would be the kind thing to do, wouldn't it? That's what it comes down to—that's the bottom line. Love is kind, heals wounds, and waits patiently. It endures anything, never retaliates, and only returns kindness.

Would you be walked on for the sake of another?

Two men going opposite directions on a narrow mountain trail meet each other head on. With a precipice on one side and sheer rock on the other, they are unable to pass. They push and squeeze, but are still unable to continue their separate journeys. Finally, without saying anything, one of the men simply lies down flat on the trail, and the other man walks over him. Now that's love. Love doesn't mind getting walked on—if it's going to benefit somebody else. That's the spirit that Paul is after in the Corinthian church. He says, "If you would only minister in a nonretaliating, self-sacrificial manner—returning kindness instead of always avenging yourself—then your spiritual gifts would mean something."

Third in this beautiful passage defining the characteristics of love is:

C. Love Is Not Jealous (v. 4c)

"Love envieth not."

Another word for *envy* is *jealousy*. Shakespeare called it "the green sickness," Solomon called it "rottenness of the bones" (Prov. 14:30b), an old Latin proverb called it "the enemy of honor," and someone else chose to call it "the sorrow of fools."

1. Jealousy dichotomized

   Now there are basically two kinds of jealousy. One is superficial, and the other is deep-down, bedrock, rotten, stinking jealousy.

   a) Superficial jealousy

   Superficial jealousy says, "I want what you have." For example, let's say my neighbor gets a new car and I respond in the following way: "Oh, I wish I had that. How come he gets a new car? How can he afford it? He doesn't make any more money than I do. People see me driving around the neighborhood in my old car, and they don't think I'm successful. And if I just get it fixed up and painted, they'll know I'm trying to *appear* successful." Superficial jealousy, then, says, "I want what he has." But that's not the deepest level.

   b) Deep-rooted jealousy

   The deepest level of jealousy says, "I wish he didn't have it." The first level of jealousy is wanting what someone else has, but the second level is resenting that he has it. William Barclay described it this way: "Meanness of the soul can sink no further than that." Deep jealousy is not just that you want something, it's that you don't want anyone else to have it.

2. Jealousy discussed

   It's easy to be jealous, isn't it? Somebody will give me a tape of someone and say, "John, you've got to hear this guy. He's fantastic!" Well, my first inclination, once I begin listening to the tape, is to say, "He's not bad, but I've heard better." But if he's really good, it's hard for me to handle, because sometimes my ego gets in the way. Now there are lots of men that are better preachers than I am—I just don't buy their tapes. That's not totally true, but you understand what I'm talking about, don't you? It's very difficult to rejoice over somebody who does exactly what you do, but does it better.

   I remember how hard it was for me as an athlete to play second string to a guy I knew was better than I was. Sometimes I wished that he'd break his leg, or I'd think, "Why did his father marry his mother and make a combination that turned out so good?" And there were times when I'd have horrible thoughts like, "Why couldn't he have had polio when he was a kid?" Jealousy causes us to say and do strange things, but it's something we all can relate to, isn't it?

3. Jealousy displayed

   The root word for *envy,* in the Greek, means "to boil." It refers to an inner boiling, seething, or steaming over something somebody else has. That is precisely what the Corinthians were doing. In 12:31a Paul says, "But covet earnestly the best gifts." In the English, it's translated as a command, but it would be better translated to read, "But you are coveting the showy gifts." Let me show you why. The Greek word for "covet" in 12:31 is the same word for "envy" in 13:4. One of the principles of hermeneutics states that when the same word is used in the same context, it means the same thing. That's why I believe that Paul is being negative in 12:31. He's not saying, "Covet certain gifts," he's saying, "The problem with you is that you're envious of certain gifts." It's the same thought. They were envious. If you doubt that, take a look at 1 Corinthians 3:3a, where Paul says, "For ye are yet carnal; for whereas there is among you envying, and strife, and divisions." They were suffering from what Solomon called "rottenness of the bones" (Prov. 14:30b).

4. Jealousy disarmed

Love does not envy. When love sees somebody who's prosperous, popular, or powerful, it is glad—it rejoices. I always think of Philippians 1:12-18, where Paul writes and says, "Yes, I'm in jail. And there are some new young preachers coming along that are being accepted by the people. These young preachers, however, are saying, 'Paul's in jail because he blew his ministry. He's not useful to the Lord, so the Lord put him on a shelf.' " In verse 16 he says, "The one preach Christ of contention, not sincerely, supposing to add affliction to my bonds." In other words, "It isn't enough that I'm in chains; they want to add more injury."

How does Paul react to them? Is he jealous that they're in the limelight? Is he jealous that they're the new breed of preachers? Is he jealous that they are doing what he used to do, only they're getting all the flowers and all the hurrahs? No. Look at his response in verse 18. "What then? . . . whether in pretense or in truth, Christ is preached; and in that I do rejoice, yea, and will rejoice." You see, Paul had the spirit that says, "I don't envy anybody who does what I do—even if they do it better and get more applause." Love just rejoices in others' success and usefulness.

5. Jealousy documented

Jealousy is such a destructive thing. I once started a little Bible study on this, and quit after only a few minutes, because I realized that it could take me a month. As I began to chart the sins that were connected to jealousy, I had a hard time getting out of Genesis. For example:

a) Eve

The first sin in the Bible is a sin of jealousy. In Genesis 3:5, Satan says to Eve, "Wouldn't you like to be like God?" Eve

55

must have thought, "Yeah, I sure would. Why should He be the only one with the knowledge of good and evil? I don't want to be left out. I want to be like God!" Jealousy spawned Eve's sin, and the race fell.

b) Cain

The next sin specifically stated in the Bible is murder. Cain killed Abel. Why? Because he was jealous—jealous of the acceptance of Abel's sacrifice over his own.

c) Joseph's brothers

I didn't get very far in Genesis until I ran into a man named Joseph whose brothers sold him into slavery. Why? Because they were jealous.

At this point in my study, I thought, "This is going to get rather lengthy—I'm still in Genesis!" Then I thought about the New Testament, and dozens of illustrations came to mind. Just one of them, for example, was about:

d) The prodigal son's brother

In Luke 15, when the prodigal son came home, the father slew the fatted calf, put a ring on his son's finger, gave him a robe, and had a party. But his older brother "was angry, and would not go" (v. 28*a*). Why? He was jealous.

6. Jealousy denounced

a) Proverbs 27:4—"Wrath is cruel, and anger is outrageous, but who is able to stand before envy?" Envy is "hatred without a cure." It destroys the insides of a man.

b) James 3:14-16—James had some words to say about jealousy and envy. "But if ye have bitter envying and strife in your hearts, glory not [i.e., you don't have anything to be proud of], and lie not against the truth. This wisdom descendeth not from above, but is earthly, sensual, demoniacal. For where envying and strife are, there is confusion and every evil work."

There it is. Every evil work spawns itself out of envy and jealousy. It's hard to conquer, isn't it? When somebody in your job gets a promotion over you, or when somebody right near you does what you do better than you, it's hard to take. I used to go through that in school. I'd work really hard, but others would get better grades than I did. And that would get me jealous. Jealousy works its way into every dimension of life. The only thing that can conquer it is love.

7. Jealousy defeated

There once was a king whose name was Saul. King Saul had a son named Jonathan, who was perhaps next in line to inherit the throne. Along came a fair-haired Hebrew singer by the name of David. And not only was he a singer, he was also a lion tamer, a giant-killer, handsome, articulate, poetic, a supreme musician—he had all kinds of abilities. One person with so much talent could be a very unpopular fellow. And with Saul, he was. Saul hated him, didn't he? He hated him because of his abilities and because of the threat that the throne could some-day go to him. One day, in a fit of fury, Saul grabbed his spear and threw it at David, trying to kill him.

Now, we don't know anything in particular about Jonathan ex-cept for the fact that he shot an arrow fairly well, right? That's about it. We don't know anything about his musical ability, or his articulation, or anything else about him. Scripture does say one important thing about him, though. Jonathan never ever had any jealousy over David. You say, "Well, he didn't stand to lose as much as Saul." Yes, he did. He was in line for the throne, and from the human perspective it could have one day been his. But the Bible says this about Jonathan, "And Jonathan . . . loved him [David] as he loved his own soul" (1 Sam. 20:17). Do you know what made the difference be-tween Saul and Jonathan? Love did. You see, Saul was jealous and Jonathan was not. Jonathan loved David, and love can't be jealous.

The Bible tells us that there's no place in the life of a Christian for jealousy—none at all. Satan's going to work on us in that area because it's such a subtle thing. We don't think it's all that evil to be jealous, but it's rotten right to the core. We all fight it. We can see the blatant, flagrant, outside sins—but the sin of jealousy can gnaw and eat at the heart from the inside.

The Subtlety of Satan's Attack on the Saints

Oscar Wilde once told a story that went something like this: The devil, while crossing the Libyan desert, came upon a group of his demons who were trying very hard to cause an old hermit to sin. Now this saintly hermit had taken his vows, been set apart by the church, said no to everything in the world, and taken his cross and gone to the desert. The demons tried to involve the hermit in sins of the flesh, tempting him in every way they knew how—but to no avail. Steadfastly, the saintly man resisted their sugges-tions. Finally, after watching their failure in disgust, the devil whispered to the demons, "What you're doing is too crude. Per-mit me one moment." And then the devil whispered to the holy man, "Your brother has just been made Bishop of Alexandria." A scowl of malignant jealousy crossed his face. "That," said the devil to his demons, "is the sort of thing I recommend."

Do you get the point? If Satan can't get us in one area, he'll get us someplace else. And jealousy is a good place to get tripped up. There's no better way to test a man than this: Let someone beneath him, or someone on his level, begin to succeed beyond him. Then see how he handles it.

How to become a fool in one easy lesson

A story is told about two great Italian symphony conductors, Toscanini and Mascagni. Mascagni was a proud, egotistical, unbelievably terrible character. Just to give you an idea of what he was like, he dedicated one of the operas he wrote to himself. Well, Mascagni resented Toscanini because of Toscanini's popularity. One day, a committee in charge of putting on a music festival in Milan (to honor the composer Verdi) inquired as to whether Toscanini and Mascagni would lead the orchestration. Mascagni was so jealous of Toscanini that he didn't even try to hide it. So he said, "I will conduct on one condition—that I am paid more money than Toscanini." The management agreed, and at the close of the festival, Mascagni received his fee—one lira. Toscanini had conducted for nothing, and Mascagni came out a fool.

A loving person rejoices in the excellence of others, in the beauty of others, in the winsomeness of others, in the success of others, and in the gifts of others. Love holds no jealousy.

When I look at Jesus, I see kindness, don't you? I see His kindness as He picks up a fallen woman and loves her. I see His long-suffering as He says on the cross, "Father, forgive them" (Luke 23:34a). And I see His total lack of jealousy as He says, "I seek not mine own glory" (John 8:50a), and instead sought to glorify His Father (John 17:4). In Matthew 20:28 He says, "Even as the Son of man came not to be ministered unto, but to minister, and to give His life a ransom for many."

So love suffers long, does deeds of kindness, and is never jealous—and there are twelve more properties (or perfections) of love to go. That's only the start.

Focusing on the Facts

1. How does 1 Corinthians 13:4-7 support the idea that love is not a feeling but an action (see p. 47)?

2. How does Paul's description of love compare to what happens when a beam of light hits a prism (see p. 48)?

3. Does Paul list the perfections of love in any particular order? Why did he list these qualities for the Corinthians (see p. 48)?

4. What is the first property of love mentioned by Paul? What is the meaning of this word, and how is it used in the New Testament (see p. 49)?

5. How did the Greek world of Paul's day view someone who was patient with people? What did they consider to be the virtuous response to any personal insult or attack? How does that compare with the perspective of our own day (see p. 49)?

6. The Greek word for patience (*makrothumeō*) literally means _____
_____ (see p. 49).

7. How do we, as Christians, know we are to be characterized by patience (see pp. 49-50)?

8. Who are some of the biblical models of patience we can follow (see p. 50)?

9. Compare kindness and patience (see pp. 51-52).

10. How is the meaning of kindness clarified by the Greek (see p. 52)?

11. Is 1 Corinthians 13:4-7 a description of how love is to behave only in ideal surroundings? Explain (see p. 52).

12. What are the two basic levels of jealousy? How do they differ in the way they express themselves (see p. 54)?

13. The root word for envy, in the Greek, means _____
(see p. 54).

14. What is the best way to translate 1 Corinthians 12:31? Why (see p. 55)?

15. What was the background to Paul's reason for rejoicing in Philippians 1:18 (see p. 55)?

16. Who was the first human to commit a sin? What was the underlying cause of this sin (see pp. 55-56)?

17. What examples can you think of, in either the Old or New Testament, of sins that are connected to jealousy (see pp. 55-56)?

18. One definition of envy, or jealousy, is "_____ without a _____" (see p. 56).

19. According to James 3:14-16, what rises out of envying and strife (see p. 56)?

20. What is the only way jealousy can be conquered (see p. 56)?

21. How did Saul and Jonathan respond differently to David? Why were their responses so different (see pp. 56-57)?

Pondering the Principles

1. The first property of love in 1 Corinthians 13 is patience, or long-suffering. It specifically refers to someone who never retaliates or gets angry when wronged by another person. It isn't a word that concerns itself with circumstances or events, it refers more to having a long fuse with people. Now the principle to ponder is this: How patient are you with the members of your family, with your colleagues at work, and with those in the body of Christ? Are you easily offended, or do you have a long fuse? Do you seek retaliation when wronged, or are you quick to forgive? If you have a problem with patience, remember this: "But the fruit of the Spirit is love, joy, peace, long-suffering" (Gal. 5:22*a*). What, then, is the only way to deal with a lack of patience? To walk in, and be filled with, the Spirit (Gal. 5:16, 25; Eph. 5:18; cf.

Col. 1:11). This involves confessing your sins (1 John 1:9), continually surrendering and submitting yourself to God, and letting "the word of Christ dwell in you richly" (Col. 3:16*a*).

2. Having evaluated patience and its presence or absence in your life, let's look at kindness. Kindness takes patience one step further and not only endures the offenses of others, but strives to meet the offender's needs. To be kind literally means "to be useful." Are you useful to others—even to your enemies (see Matt. 5:43-48)? When someone hurts you or gets angry at you, is your first thought to do something kind for them? Do you think that others characterize you as being kind? Ask God to make you into a man or woman of kindness, and ask Him to show you practical ways to be useful to those around you.

3. Is there somebody who does the same thing that you do—whether it's your job, your ministry, your sport, or your hobby—but they do it better? How do you feel about that person? Do you admire someone who is better than you at what you both do, or are you jealous over their expertise? When a friend gets something that you have had your eyes on for a long time, but you couldn't (and still can't) afford, do you become genuinely happy for them, or do you become disappointed and feel sorry for yourself? Do you even get jealous over someone who owns more than you, is more attractive than you, has a better job than you, is more eloquent than you, is smarter than you, is thinner than you, wears nicer clothes than you, drives a more expensive car than you, has more friends than you, has a happier marriage than you, gets better grades than you, and so on? At what level does your jealousy usually manifest itself—superficial (wanting what they have) or deep-rooted (not wanting them to have what they have)? All jealousy is wrong and needs to be confessed as sin. However, the deeper level of jealousy is much more destructive, and more indicative of the sin of discontentment. Honestly evaluate your life in terms of jealousy or discontentment, and confess all of it to God. Then read and meditate on Philippians 4:11-12 and 1 Timothy 6:6-11.

4
The Qualities of True Love—
Part 2

Outline

Introduction
A. Paul's Portrait of Christ Communicated
B. Paul's Portrait of Christ Contrasted

Review
I. The Prominence of Love
II. The Perfections of Love
  A. Love Is Patient
  B. Love Is Kind
  C. Love Is Not Jealous

Lesson
  D. Love Is Not Boastful
    1. The definition of boastfulness
    2. The description of boastfulness
    3. The display of boastfulness
    4. The desire of boastfulness
    5. The denial of boastfulness
  E. Love Is Not Conceited
    1. The practice of being puffed up
      a) The conceited composer
      b) The conceited congregation
        (1) Their past teaching
        (2) Their supposed spiritual state
        (3) Their sexual accomplishments
        (4) Their biblical knowledge
    2. The Proverbs against pride
      a) Proverbs 8:13
      b) Proverbs 11:2*a*
      c) Proverbs 13:10*a*
      d) Proverbs 16:18
      e) Proverbs 29:23*a*
  F. Love Is Not Rude
    1. The extent of the Corinthians' rudeness

61

    a) The love feast
    b) The Lord's Table
    c) The women
    d) The glossolalists
G. Love Is Not Selfish
  1. The Corinthians' selfishness
  2. Christ's selflessness
H. Love Is Not Provoked
  1. Spiritual anger
  2. Self-centered anger

Introduction

A. Paul's Portrait of Christ Communicated

The thirteenth chapter of 1 Corinthians is a portrait of love. It comes out, however, as a portrait of Jesus Christ, because He is love. Christ would like to reproduce His portrait in us and to have His church be a collection of reprints. As we are studying the qualities of love in 1 Corinthians 13:4-7 and examining the portrait of Christ, He is looking at us to see if His portrait is being reprinted and reproduced in us.

Now, the apostle Paul is pointing out to the Corinthians what love is. In our last lesson we saw that love is something that can't be defined philosophically or ideologically; one can only describe how it functions. In fact, the Bible doesn't define love; it only describes it in action. In verses 4-7, Paul uses verbs to describe how love acts, rather than defining love with adjectives.

This chapter is the greatest, most far-reaching, broad description of love that has ever been penned by the Holy Spirit's inspiration. It's tremendously and intensely practical. And even though it's a portrait of Jesus Christ, which gives it an exalted character, it is at the same time a shoe-leather presentation of what Christ wants to reproduce in us in our daily living.

B. Paul's Portrait of Christ Contrasted

It's important to understand that the portrait Paul is presenting is in contrast to the behavior of the Corinthians. They didn't have love—and were actually the opposite of love—so Paul had to describe love's characteristics to them. I'm afraid, however, that we're no better. We need to hear what Paul is saying and examine our own lives.

Basically, what Paul is saying is this: "Love is very patient, but we are mostly impatient. Love is very kind, but we are frequently unkind. Love knows no jealousy, but we are often jealous. Love makes no parade, but we are proud. Love is never rude, but we are often rude and ill mannered. Love is never selfish, but we are mostly self-centered. Love never gets irritated, but we are short-tempered very often. Love is never resentful, but we seem to look for slights and wrongs and make note of it. Love is never glad when someone else goes wrong, but we often take secret delight in someone else's failure. Love is gladdened by goodness and is always slow to expose and eager to believe the best, but we are often judgmental." That's the approach Paul's taking. He's putting all the positives of love against the negatives of the Corinthian assembly. And remember, since we are no better than the Corinthians when we're in the flesh, we are being contrasted as well.

When man was created, he was created in the image of God. And since God's love was his by possession, all these characteristics belonged to him. But when the Fall came, all of it was lost. Once the image of God was marred, love was marred, and man became loveless. Unregenerate man, as well as a Christian functioning in the flesh, is loveless. So Paul details for us what love is to be.

Review

I. The Prominence of Love (vv. 1-3; see pp. 12-21, 29-42)

II. The Perfections of Love (vv. 4-7)
    A. Love Is Patient (v. 4*a*; see pp. 49-51)
    B. Love Is Kind (v. 4*b*; see pp. 51-53)
    C. Love Is Not Jealous (v. 4*c*; see pp. 53-58)

Lesson

    D. Love Is Not Boastful (v. 4*d*)

    "Love vaunteth not itself."

    1. The definition of boastfulness

You'll notice that the phrase "love vaunteth not itself" is followed by the statement "is not puffed up." Now those statements may seem like synonyms or parallels, but they aren't. There's a difference. The first statement represents the verbalizing of pride, the actual speech of pride, the actual action of pride. The second statement represents the attitude of pride—conceit that is down inside.

The Greek word that tells us love is not boastful comes from a root word meaning "windbag." Boastfulness is just the verbalizing, the windbag, the hot air that comes out of the mouth of a proud, conceited person. Incidentally, this word is used only once in the entire New Testament—right here in this verse. Love is not a windbag. Love is not always shooting off its mouth about its own accomplishments. Love does not speak an arrogant, baseless chatter that is designed to make me look better than you.

Bragging is an effort to make other people feel inferior because of what you are or what you have. In other words, it is the flip side of envy. Notice, in verse 4, that he says, "Love doesn't envy," and then turns it around and says, "Love doesn't brag." Envy is wanting something that other people have, and bragging is making people want what you have.

2. The description of boastfulness

You know how it works. While somebody is telling a marvelous story about some accomplishment, you're half-listening and dying for them to get done so you can say, "Well, if you think that's something, let me tell you about what I did!" and off you go. Then a third party chimes in and tries to do even better. The whole idea of bragging is to make somebody else feel that you are superior to them. But that is the opposite of love, isn't it? Love says, "I want you to feel superior. I'll take the role of a servant." Love never brags or blows its own horn. And let's face it, nobody really likes people who do, because they are loveless people. When I'm around somebody like that, I don't want to fellowship with them. I'd rather leave—or I wish they would.

3. The display of boastfulness

The Corinthians were a bunch of spiritual show-offs. They were totally inconsiderate of each other and constantly vying for public attention. The Corinthian church services were chaotic, with everybody talking at the same time and vying for the rulership. There is no mention in the entire Corinthians letter of an elder. They didn't even have any leaders. And as far as we know, nobody had responsibility. We don't know what kind of organization their church had (if any), but it was absolute chaos. Look at 1 Corinthians 14:26. Paul says, "How is it, then, brethren? When ye come together, every one of you hath a psalm, hath a doctrine, hath a tongue, hath a revelation, hath an interpretation." What kind of chaos is that? Everybody was a spiritual show-off, and everybody wanted to do his own thing, so there was bragging and a constant vying for public attention.

4. The desire of boastfulness

I don't know if you realize it, but boasting is geared to hurt other people. It is geared to wound somebody else—to make *you* stand out and *them* look inferior. It's easy to do. I have to be careful about this, especially when I talk to other pastors—dear men of God who are faithfully serving the Lord. When someone comes along like myself, to whom God has given the very unusual privilege of being able to pastor a church that's large and complex, these men are tempted to feel like failures. Why? Because there's too much propaganda going around today saying that if it isn't big, it isn't good. But that's a big lie! Big doesn't mean anything—except that it's big. People say, "Well, you have four thousand members in your church." That's true, but ninety-two thousand people show up at the

L.A. Coliseum to watch men run around with a piece of pig. The fact that something is big doesn't mean anything at all. But it's very easy, when you're in the kind of position that I'm in, to be tempted to make other people feel inferior.

We all have at least one thing that we can do fairly well. And whatever it is, we usually let a few folks know about it, don't we? Boasting is nothing more than blinding self-centeredness—the desire to make somebody else envy. It's a sin not only because it's a wrong thing to do, but because it makes somebody else jealous. Boasting makes your brother stumble.

Are you always the topic of your conversations?

I remember when I was in my first year of seminary. As I was trying to orient my life, I got ahold of a book by H. Clay Trumbull called *Principles of Evangelism*. He made a statement in that book that has stuck with me all these years. He said, "I made a vow to God to change my life. My vow was this: God, if You'll give me the strength, every time I have the opportunity to introduce the topic of conversation, it will always be of Jesus Christ."

When we open our mouths, what we say ought to be of Jesus Christ—not us. And once we learn to do that, we'll get away from always talking about ourselves. I hear pastors, radio speakers, and Christian television personalities who do nothing but talk about themselves, what they have done, and what they have accomplished. That can get very intimidating.

C. S. Lewis called boasting "the utmost evil . . . the greatest sin . . . the essential vice (i.e., the vice at the very essence of man)." There's no place for it in the life of a Christian.

5. The denial of boastfulness

Look at the pattern of Jesus Christ. If anybody had anything to brag about, He certainly did. But you never find Him doing that. In studying the gospel of John, which presents His deity, it's amazing to see how many times Jesus denies the opportunity to boast. For example, in John 12:49*a*, Jesus says, "For I have not spoken of myself; but the Father, who sent me." How many of you can say that? How many of you at the end of one day can say, "God, I have not spoken of myself today"? We should be able to say that!

Only love can save us from flaunting our knowledge, our ability, our education, our gifts, or ourselves. Love is not boastful. But at the root of boasting is a sin that Paul addresses next in his list of the qualities of love.

E. Love Is Not Conceited (v. 4*e*)

"Love . . . is not puffed up."

1. The practice of being puffed up

    a) The conceited composer

    In the last lesson, I told you about Mascagni, the great composer who wrote an opera that he dedicated to himself. The opera, entitled *The Masks,* was dedicated with the following words: "To myself, with distinguished esteem and unalterable satisfaction." That's quite a commentary on the misery of that man's soul, isn't it? Conceit goes deeper than the mouth. There is bragging—the hot air, the shooting off of one's mouth—and then there is deep-down conceit.

    b) The conceited congregation

    When Paul told the Corinthians that love is not puffed up, he was really telling them they had no love. Why? Because they were really puffed up. They saw themselves as spiritual hotshots. They thought that they had arrived. They felt that they had all the answers. Let me show you some of the specific things that they were puffed up about.

    (1) Their past teaching

    In 4:18 Paul says, "Now some are puffed up, as though I would not come to you." Why would they think that? They were probably thinking, "Why would Paul come here? We have it all—we already know everything. There's nothing that Paul can tell us that we haven't already heard. We've had the best teachers—Paul, Apollos, and Cephas—what more do we need? Paul will never show up around here."

    Not only were they puffed up about the knowledge they had received from certain teachers, they were also puffed up about:

    (2) Their supposed spiritual state

    Let's look at 4:6-10. "And these things, brethren, I have in a figure transferred to myself and to Apollos for your sakes [i.e., I'm using myself and Apollos as an illustration], that ye might learn in us [as models or illustrations] not to think of men above that which is written, that no one of you be puffed up for one against another." In other words, Paul says, "You better take a biblical evaluation of yourself, and stop being puffed up." In verse 7 he says, "For who maketh thee to differ from another? And what hast thou that thou didst not receive? Now if you didst receive it, why dost thou glory, as if thou hadst not received it?" In spite of the fact that they had nothing to boast about, in spite of the fact that everything they received was a gift from God, and in spite of the fact that God was the One who had made them different, they were still thinking too highly of themselves.

66

In verse 8, Paul gets sarcastic and says, "Now ye are full, now ye are rich, ye have reigned as kings without us [i.e., You think you're really something!]; and I would to God ye did reign, that we also might reign with you. For I think that God hath set forth us, the apostles, last." Then, getting very sarcastic, he says, in verse 10, "We are fools for Christ's sake, but ye are wise in Christ; we are weak, but ye are strong; ye are honorable, but we are despised." They were bragging about their supposed spiritual state, but the fact of the matter was they were in gross, gross carnality.

Further, the Corinthians were puffed up about:

(3) Their sexual accomplishments

In 5:1 Paul says, "It is reported commonly that there is fornication [Gk., *porneia,* "sexual sin"] among you, and such fornication as is not so much as named among the Gentiles [or "heathen"], that one should have his father's wife [incest]." And what was their attitude? Look at verse 2: "And ye are puffed up." They were even conceited about their sexual accomplishments.

(4) Their biblical knowledge

Look at 8:1. "Now as touching things offered unto idols, we know that we all have knowledge [i.e., "We all understand the reality about meat offered to idols"]. Knowledge puffeth up, but love edifieth [builds up]."

They were puffed up about their biblical knowledge. They were puffed up about their sexual accomplishments. They were puffed up about their supposed spiritual status. They were puffed up about the certain teachers they had followed. They were egotistical and conceited about the spiritual gifts they had, which they were using to dominate other people. And they had an inner arrogance that spawned mouths full of hot air. Can you imagine an entire congregation of these people?

Love is not puffed up. Do you know why? Because conceit says, "I'm better than you," but love says just the opposite. Conceit says, "I want everybody to know all about me," but love says, "I wish I could know all about you."

The Impossibility of Humiliating a Humble Person

William Carey was one of the greatest missionaries who ever lived and one of the greatest linguists the world has ever seen—Christian or non-Christian. William Carey translated parts of the Bible into no fewer than thirty-four different Indian languages. He began his life as a cobbler, fixing shoes. When he arrived in India as a missionary, he was immediately regarded with dislike and contempt because of the very stringent caste system that the people had been locked into for centuries. So he was given absolutely no respect.

One time, at a dinner party that Carey was attending, a snob had the idea of humiliating Carey because of Carey's low estate. So that all could hear, he said, "I hear, Mr Carey, that you once worked as a shoemaker?" "Oh no, your lordship," said William Carey, "not a shoemaker, only a shoe repairman." He wouldn't even claim that he made shoes if he only repaired them. Somebody once said, "Empty trucks make the most noise."

2. The proverbs against pride

Proverbs tells us much about pride and bragging. For example:

a) Proverbs 8:13—"the fear of the Lord is to hate evil; pride, and arrogance . . . do I hate."

b) Proverbs 11:2a—"When pride cometh, then cometh shame."

c) Proverbs 13:10a—"Only by pride cometh contention." That's so true. All that pride ever does is breed contention and start fights. That's all it ever does. Humility has never started a fight yet. Humble people don't have anything to argue about. They just give. Proud people are contentious and start fights.

d) Proverbs 16:18—"Pride goeth before destruction, and an haughty spirit before a fall." That's just pointing out that proud people are always the most ignorant of all, because in their pride and smugness they don't understand what awaits them.

e) Proverbs 29:23a—"A man's pride shall bring him low." Love is not bigheaded, love is bighearted.

For a period of time prior to Jesus' ministry, John the Baptist was a hero, a great prophet out in the wilderness. Masses of people came to him day after day. One day, John's disciples were questioning him about Jesus, and he replied, "He must increase, but I must decrease" (John 3:30). In other words, "The sooner you forget about John the Baptist, the better I'm going to like it." Now that's humility!

Now, what have we seen so far? Love is the only hope for the Corinthians—and for us, as well. This love is superior to eloquence, to spiritual insight, to knowledge, to faith, to charity, and to martyrdom. This love suffers long and is kind. And it's the only power in the world that can save us from the stupid swagger of boastfulness and from indulging in the sneers of envy. "Love never begrudges," says Paul, "and never shows off."

In verse 5, Paul gives us a sixth quality of love.

F. Love Is Not Rude (v. 5a)

"[Love] doth not behave itself unseemly."

Love doesn't behave rudely. That is so practical. The verb here means "to behave in an unbecoming manner." It refers to poor manners—rudeness. You say, "Well, that seems rather minor, doesn't it? Is rudeness all tied up with agape, the great concept of divine love?" Yes, it is. Someone with poor manners and rudeness is saying, "I don't love you, because I could care less what affects you. I will do what I want whether you like it or not."

Slurping and Burping

When I was a little kid my mom was constantly telling me, "Don't slurp your soup!" I used to think, "Who cares if I slurp my soup?" Then one time I ate with somebody who slurped his soup. I wasn't really able to enjoy mine while he was enjoying his. At that point, I finally realized that not slurping my soup had nothing to do with keeping my clothes clean, it had something to do with how much other folks could enjoy their time at the table. It's a little thing that says, "Your happiness matters to me, so I want to do what makes you happy."

I knew a couple who got an annulment on the grounds that he was rude to his wife. It's the strangest thing you've ever heard. She went to court and claimed that he burped all the time. That's the truth! I actually knew the people. Well, the judge granted an annulment on the basis that it was apparent the man did not love the woman, or he would have been more considerate of her than to burp all the time. Now that's an extreme story, but it illustrates the point. Love is not rude.

The literal meaning of the verb here is "to be shapeless or unformed." So it's not only referring to unbecoming behavior, it's also referring to undisciplined behavior. This describes a person, a man or a woman, who doesn't have the ability to discipline his behavior with others in mind. He's just rude, out of place, overbearing, and totally self-centered.

1. The extent of the Corinthians' rudeness

There couldn't be a better definition of the Corinthians than the word *rude*. They couldn't care less about anybody else. For example:

a) The love feast—They were so rude that they came to the love feast and ate all their own food before the people who had none got there. They overindulged. They were like hogs when it came to eating at the love feast.

b) The Lord's Table—Their behavior at the Lord's Table was so bad that they got drunk because they kept taking the cup.

c) The women—Women had overstepped the bounds of female propriety before God. They were taking their veils off and usurping the role of men in the church. They were, therefore, not acting in a becoming way.

d) The glossolalists—The undisciplined, rude conduct of the Corinthian glossalalists had come to the place where it was the antithesis of love. Everybody was shouting out and trying to get the prominence without considering anyone else. And when you do that there's no love there. Love is never rude, because love is always lost in how it affects somebody else.

2. The example of Christ's love

Our dear Lord was so tremendous in personifying love. Luke 7 shows us an incident where the Lord protected a woman from someone else's rudeness. Beginning in verse 36 it says, "And one of the Pharisees desired him that he would eat with him. And he went into the Pharisee's house, and sat down to eat. And, behold, a woman in the city, who was a sinner [undoubtedly a prostitute], when she knew that Jesus was eating in the Pharisee's house, brought an alabaster box of ointment [which was extremely expensive], and stood at his feet behind him, weeping; and began to wash his feet with tears, and did wipe them with the hair of her head, and kissed his feet, and anointed them with the ointment." Isn't that beautiful? That prostitute is weeping, washing Jesus' feet with her tears, wiping them with her hair, and putting ointment on them.

Continuing on in verse 39, "Now when the Pharisee who had bidden him saw it, he spoke within himself, saying, This man, if He were a prophet [he hasn't made his evaluation of Christ yet], would have known who and what manner of woman this is that toucheth him; for she is a sinner. And Jesus, answering, said unto him [notice that Jesus answered his thought], Simon, I have somewhat to say unto thee. And he saith, Master, say on." What a hypocrite! He hadn't even made up his mind whether or not Jesus was Master.

In response to Simon's rude thoughts, Jesus told the following parable, beginning in verse 41: "There was a certain creditor who had two debtors: the one owed five hundred denarii, and the other fifty. And when they had nothing to pay, he frankly forgave them both. Tell me, therefore, which of them will love him most? Simon answered, and said, I suppose that he to whom he forgave most. And He said unto him, Thou hast rightly judged. And He turned to the woman, and said unto Simon, Seest thou this woman? I entered into thine house; thou gavest me no water for my feet. But she hath washed my feet with tears, and wiped them with the hair of her head. Thou gavest me no kiss. But this woman, since the time I came in, hath not ceased to kiss my feet. My head with oil thou didst not anoint. But this woman hath anointed my feet with ointment. Wherefore, I say unto thee, her sins, which are many, are forgiven; for she loved much. But to whom little is forgiven, the same loveth little." There's a lot of sarcasm in that statement, isn't there? "And He said unto her, Thy sins are forgiven. And they that were eating with him began to say within themselves, Who is this that forgiveth sins also? And he said to the woman, Thy faith hath saved thee; go in peace."

You say, "What's the story teaching?" It shows us a very simple principle. A woman, who in all likelihood was a prostitute, entered a Pharisee's home. The first response of the Pharisee to that woman would have been rude, arrogant, and scornful. He would have said, "What are you doing in here, you filthy, vile, sinning woman? Get out!" But Jesus shielded the woman from the Pharisee's scorn, arrogance, rudeness, and indifference. And Jesus loved her, forgave her, and redeemed her.

Are you rude to unbelieving people?

William Barclay translates the first part of 1 Corinthians 13:5 in the following way: "Love does not behave gracelessly." Love is gracious—never rude. And it isn't just a matter of whether or not you're rude to a believer; love is never even rude to an unbeliever. I've seen some Christians who were so rude to non-Christians who smoked that they would never have an opportunity to communicate something about Christ. Once we get to the place where we think we understand all the doctrine, and we think we have all the answers, we will become theological hardheads who have no grace or charm with people who aren't where we are. That isn't right! We can shut out everyone who isn't just like us and say, "Us four, no more, shut the door," without any grace or kindness. But that's rude, isn't it? I believe that Christianity very often has to pay the price for its rudeness to unbelieving people. Oftentimes, we are very rude and thoughtless to people. And wrongly so, because love is not rude!

So love can save us from the bitter sneer of envy on the one hand and the ridiculous swagger of boastfulness on the other. Love can also save us from the inner tendency to be so inflated with our own importance that we're rude to everybody else—behaving without grace, in contempt of them and their feelings.

Seventh in Paul's list of the qualities of love is:

G. Love Is Not Selfish (v. 5*b*)

"[Love] seeketh not its own."

71

Love isn't interested in its own things; it's interested in the things of someone else. Lenski, the great commentator, said this: "Cure selfishness and you plant a garden of Eden." He's right. I would say that in Paul's portrait of love, selflessness represents the eyes. The windows of the soul show the soul to be selfless.

1. The Corinthians' selfishness

The Corinthians were extremely selfish—especially as it related to their spiritual gifts. In fact, if you studied the combination of the Greek words in verse 5 and compared them with the Greek construction of 14:4, you would see an amazing comparison. In 13:5 Paul basically says, "Stop being selfish and seeking that which is your own." Then in 14:4, as he talks to them about their use of the gift of tongues, he says, "He that speaketh in an unknown tongue edifieth himself." Now, because of the similar construction in those two verses, it's possible that in 13:5 Paul is speaking directly to the Corinthians' problem of seeking self-edification as seen in 14:4. In fact, this is further substantiated by 14:12b, where Paul says, "Seek that ye may excel to the edifying of the church." The Corinthians had twisted the purpose of spiritual gifts. Instead of using their gifts for others, they were using their own gifts to individually build themselves up. But love is free from that. Love never dwells on itself.

The Best Way to Help Yourself Is to Help Others

Fulton Oursler, some years ago, told the following story: A uniformed chauffeur approached the desk of a clerk in a cemetery and said, "The lady is too ill to walk. Would you mind coming with me?" Waiting in the car was a frail, elderly woman whose sunken eyes could not hide some deep, long-lasting hurt. "I'm Mrs. So-and-so," she said weakly. "Every week for the last two years I have been sending you a five-dollar bill in the mail." "Oh yes—for the flowers!" the clerk remembered. "Yes, to be laid on the grave of my loved one. I came today," she confided softly, "because the doctors have let me know I have only a few weeks left. I shall not be sorry to go. There's nothing to live for anyway, so I wanted to drive for one last look at the grave."

The clerk blinked at her irresolutely. Then with a wry smile he spoke, "You know, ma'am, I'm very sorry you kept sending the money for the flowers." "Sorry?" she asked. "Yes," he replied. "The flowers last such a little while, and no one ever sees them." "Do you realize what you're saying?" she asked. "Oh, indeed I do. You see, I belong to a visiting society," he said. "I go to state hospitals and insane asylums, where people dearly love flowers—and they can see them and smell them. Lady, there are living people in places like that." The woman sat in silence for a moment, and then, without a word, she signaled the chauffeur to drive away.

Some months later, the clerk was astonished to receive another visit. Only this time he was doubly astonished, because the woman was driving the car. "I take the flowers to the people at the hospitals myself," she said with a friendly smile. "You were right! It does make them happy; and it makes me happy, too. The doctors don't know what is making me well—but I do. I have somebody else to live for."

She had discovered what most of us know and too often forget—in helping others, she had helped herself. Paul put it this way: "Bear ye one another's burdens, and so fulfill the law of Christ" (Gal. 6:2).

2. Christ's selflessness

Jesus is the perfect example of selflessness. Matthew 20:28 says, "Even as the Son of man came not to be ministered unto, but to minister, and to give his life a ransom for many." Love never seeks its own, it's always seeking the good of somebody else.

I believe that selflessness is the key to the whole concept of love as described by Paul in 1 Corinthians 13. If you're patient with people, kind with people, not jealous of people, not angry with people, not upset with people, not easily provoked by people, very tolerant with people, very generous with people, very gracious with people, and never rude to people—you're selfless.

Eighth in Paul's description of love is:

H. Love Is Not Provoked (v. 5c)

"[Love] is not easily provoked."

The Greek word translated "provoked" is *paroxunō*. It is from this word that we get our English word *paroxysm,* which means "a sudden outburst." In other words, love never gets upset, irritated, or angry. Love is never ready to fight.

1. Spiritual anger

You say, "Wait a minute! If love doesn't get provoked, how do you explain righteous indignation?" Well, if you're cleansing the Temple, go right ahead. It's all right. I'm sure Martin Luther was a little angry when he nailed his Ninety-five Theses on the door of the church at Wittenberg. I'm all for it. In fact, you can't really live the Christian life without a little bit of anger. You have to be mad at Satan, you have to be mad at the flesh, and you have to be angry with what defiles God's world and God's truth, don't you? That's righteous indignation— which I believe every man of God has to have.

73

Competition and the Preacher

Dr. Haddon Robinson once told me that he has never met a preacher who was any good, who wasn't competitive and always in a fight. I asked him what he meant before I agreed with him, and this is what he said: "A preacher who isn't competitive isn't going to be a good preacher of the Word of God week after week after week." Well, I agree with that. I'll use myself as an illustration. I'm very competitive. I like to win—I've always been that way. I did spend a lot of my life losing, but I never did like it. I like to win because I'm competitive. You say, "How does that relate to preaching?" Well, in the same way that a blind dog will stumble over a bone once in a while, every preacher is going to preach one or two good sermons. That's just a law of averages. Every preacher will find a good truth every now and then. However, to be good week after week after week, you have to be a fighter—you have to be competitive. You have to fight the clock, you have to fight your own ignorance, you have to fight the difficulties in the text, you have to fight the people who try to change your priorities, you have to fight your own laziness, you have to fight your own sin—it's an all-out war! But Sunday is victory day. Do you know why I get so excited when I preach? The fight for the week is over. It takes me a lot of time to prepare the message, and being competitive certainly helps.

I'm not depreciating the fact that there is, in the Christian life, a need to get irritated about certain things. But what Paul is saying in 1 Corinthians 13:5 is that love doesn't get mad, angry, and upset at other people.

2. Self-centered anger

Next time you get mad or upset at home, remember this: You're angry because you don't love the one you're angry at. When you get angry, what you say often wounds the other person. But that's because you want to wound and hurt them. When you get angry, you decide, "I want my way, and I want it the way I want it. And if you don't do it the way I want it, I'm going to hurt you." Anger causes us to say things that will never be forgotten—things that leave deep scars. We do things that hurt and injure, but love bears all injuries. Love suffers everything without irritation and exasperation, unless it's defending God. But when it comes to defending yourself, love is not provoked.

When a husband lashes out and punches his wife, does he love her? Absolutely not! He doesn't love her. He is more concerned about himself than anything else. So if she crosses him, he lets her know about it. What do you do if your child does something that you don't like? Does that frail little baby become a battered child? Does your child get knocked across the room into the wall because he does something that stepped on what you thought you wanted for yourself? Well, that's anger. Anger is the opposite of love because anger says, "I matter so much, if you do something that I don't like, I'm going to let you have it."

Anger is not an easy thing to handle, but unless you learn to handle it, you'll never really experience love. You can constantly tell your husband you love him, but if all you ever do is get angry at him, it's going to be very hard to convince him of it. You can tell your children you love them, but if all you ever do is yell at them, get irritated at them, and get upset at them, they're going to wonder why they can't ever do anything that makes you happy—and it's going to be hard to convince them of your love. Love is the only cure for irritability, because irritability, in the last analysis, is simply self-centeredness.

The Consequences of an Uncontrollable Temper

Jonathan Edwards, the third president of Princeton University, and one of the greatest preachers of history, had a daughter with an uncontrollable temper. A young man fell in love with her, but because their courting was all hearts and flowers, he was unaware of her temper. The day finally arrived when the young man went to the girl's father to ask for her hand in marriage. "Dr. Edwards," he said, "I want to marry your daughter." "You can't have her," was the abrupt answer of Jonathan Edwards. "But I love her," replied the young man. "You still can't have her," Edwards repeated. "But she loves me!" argued the young man. "You still can't have her," Edwards again repeated. "But why not?" the exasperated young man pleaded. "Because she's not worthy of you," Edwards answered. Astonished, the young man asked, "But, Dr. Edwards, she's a Christian, isn't she?" "Yes," said Edwards, "but the grace of God can live with some people with whom no one else could ever live." His daughter was like the lady who said, "I lose my temper, but it's all over in a minute." So is the atom bomb!

I could talk a lot about temper and how it can destroy a person, but the point that Paul is making here is simply this: Being provoked—getting angry—isn't loving.

Consider the following. As a Christian, the love of God is shed abroad in your heart. Jesus personified love, and Paul modeled it. Are you following these examples, or are you carnal like the Corinthians—seeing yourself as the opposite of all these qualities of love?

Focusing on the Facts

1. Why is 1 Corinthians 13 seen as a portrait of Jesus Christ (see p. 62)?

2. How can we benefit from studying 1 Corinthians 13 (see pp. 62-63)?

3. The end of 1 Corinthians 13:4 says, "Love vaunteth not itself, is not puffed up." What is the difference between these two qualities of love (see p. 63)?

4. The Greek word for boastfulness comes from a root word which means " _____ " (see p. 63).

5. _____ is wanting something that other people have, and _____ is making people want what you have (see p. 64).

6. What is the underlying motive behind boastfulness (see p. 64)?

7. What was chaotic about the Corinthian worship service? Why was it that way (see p. 64)?

8. How are boastfulness and conceit connected (see p. 66)?

9. What does it mean to be "puffed up"? In what areas were the Corinthians puffed up (see pp. 66-67)?

10. What are some of the consequences of pride, according to Proverbs 11:2; 13:10; 16:18; and 29:23 (see p. 68)?

11. Why is John the Baptist such a great example of humility (see p. 68)?

12. What does it mean that love does "not behave itself unseemly" (see p. 69)?

13. When people are rude, what are they basically saying to those that they are rude to (see p. 69)?

14. In what ways were the Corinthians rude (see pp. 69-70)?

15. What lesson can we learn from Luke 7:36-50 (see pp. 70-71)?

16. Are Christians ever justified in being rude to unbelievers (see p. 71)?

17. How were the Corinthians selfish as it related to their spiritual gifts (see p. 72)?

18. Why is it important for us to bear one another's burdens (see p. 73)?

19. How is Christ the absolute example of selflessness (see p. 73)?

20. Explain why selflessness could be considered the key to the concept of love described in 1 Corinthians 13 (see p. 73).

21. What does it mean to be provoked? Should Christians ever get provoked? Explain (see pp. 73-74).

22. Why is it important for an effective preacher to be competitive (see p. 74)?

23. Explain the difference between spiritual anger and self-centered anger (see pp. 74-75).

24. Can a person love someone and at the same time be constantly angry with them? Explain (see p. 75).

25. What is the only cure for irritability (see p. 75)?

Pondering the Principles

1. When was the last time you were involved in boasting about yourself? What was the content of your boast? Why did you boast? Do you boast frequently? When someone is telling a story about something that they have done, do you usually chime in with a story to better theirs? If so, why? Everybody has at least one thing that they do fairly well. What are you good at? Do you make it a point to let others know about it? Answer these questions honestly, and then ask God to make you sensitive to those times when you are prone to boast. Commit yourself to being able to say at the end of one day, "God, I have not spoken of myself today."

2. Do you enjoy being around someone who is conceited and boastful? Why or why not? Has anyone ever accused you of being conceited? Did you feel falsely accused? If so, did you ask your accuser why they felt that way? Was their perception of you based on a misunderstanding, or did God use them to show you a problem area in your life that you were previously blind to? The apostle Paul was certainly someone who could have become proud. However, look at the following passages: 1 Corinthians 1:26-2:5; 15:9-10; 2 Corinthians 3:5; 10:7-18; 11:16-30; 12:6-10; Philippians 3:3-10; 1 Timothy 1:15.

3. One of the qualities of love is that it is not rude. How would you define rudeness? Think of some illustrations of rude behavior that you personally have received. What was your response to those acts of rudeness? Can you think of times when you were rude? What prompted your rudeness? Oftentimes, people who would never think of being rude to strangers are habitually rude to their family and loved ones. Is that true in your own life? Why is that so often true? Another problem is that Christians are often extremely rude to non-Christians. Is our love to be limited just to Christians? Why, then, do many Christians feel that their rudeness is justified? Ask God to make you more aware of the times when you are rude and to be sensitive to how your actions and words affect others—Christian or non-Christian.

4. Selflessness could very well be considered the key to love as described by Paul in 1 Corinthians 13. List the fifteen qualities of love from verses 4-7 and then determine how selflessness relates to each one.

5. There is a place for anger in the life of every Christian. Paul said, "Be ye angry, and sin not" (Eph. 4:26a). This anger that Paul is referring to is a righteous anger—anger that is designed to defend the great, glorious, holy nature of God. However, in the same verse and the next, Paul also says, "Let not the sun go down upon your wrath; neither give place to the devil." You can be angry over that which grieves God, but you're not to get angry when people offend you. Anger that is self-centered, undisciplined, and uncontrolled is sinful, useless, and hurtful—and it must be confessed and dealt with before it's slept on. "Why?" you ask. Because anger that isn't dealt with

gives Satan victory in your life. You ought to be angry over sin—especially sin in the church—but your anger must never degenerate into sin. Commit yourself to get angry over only that which offends God, never over that which offends you. Also, make it a habit to deal with your anger (or any sin) quickly, so that Satan won't get an advantage over you (2 Cor. 2:11).

5
The Qualities of True Love—
Part 3

Outline

Introduction

Review
I. The Prominence of Love
II. The Perfections of Love
    A. Love Is Patient
    B. Love Is Kind
    C. Love Is Not Jealous
    D. Love Is Not Boastful
    E. Love Is Not Conceited
    F. Love Is Not Rude
    G. Love Is Not Selfish
    H. Love Is Not Provoked
        1. Spiritual anger
        2. Self-centered anger

Lesson
        a) The defense of personal rights
        b) The duty to practice love
I. Love Thinks No Evil
    1. *Logizomai* defined
    2. *Logizomai* discussed
        a) What is not imputed
            (1) Romans 4:8
            (2) 2 Corinthians 5:19*a*
        b) What is imputed
            (1) Romans 4:6
            (2) Romans 4:22
            (3) James 2:23*a*
J. Love Does Not Rejoice in Unrighteousness
    1. The ways to rejoice in sin
        a) Rejoicing in your own sin
        b) Rejoicing in somebody else's sin
            (1) The salability of newspapers

        (2) The search for legitimate grounds
    2. The wrongness of rejoicing in sin
       a) How it affronts God
       b) How it affects sinners
    3. The wagging tongue that rejoices in sin
K. Love Rejoices with the Truth
    1. Its basis
       a) Identified
       b) Illustrated
    2. Its benefits

Introduction

It is said that in a churchyard near the old village of Leamington, England, there stands a tombstone with the following inscription: "Here lies a miser who lived for himself, and cared for nothing but gathering wealth; now where he is or how he fares, nobody knows and nobody cares." In contrast, there's a plain tombstone at St. Paul's Cathedral in London with an inscription that reads, "Sacred to the memory of General Charles George Gordon, who at all times and everywhere gave his strength to the weak, his substance to the poor, his sympathy to the suffering, his heart to God."

Two epitaphs—two distinct opposites. One life shows lovelessness, the other life shows love. And really, in the last analysis of it all, the only people who really contribute to the world are the unselfish ones. Stated another way, the only time anybody contributes is when they do something that is unselfish. The only useful people in the world are those who have given their strength to the weak, their substance to the poor, their sympathy to the suffering, and their hearts to God. That's what love does.

I don't know what the commentary's going to be on my life. I've often thought that the smart thing to do would be to write my own epitaph, like Benjamin Franklin, so they have to put it on my tombstone. But certainly it would be tragic if at the time of our death it was made public that we were spending our entire life flaunting our selfishness. Nothing is sufficient in the life of a Christian except love. It must take a prominent place.

Review

I. The Prominence of Love (vv. 1-3; see pp. 12-21, 29-42)

The Corinthian assembly didn't have love, so Paul had to write some strong words to them. The Corinthians had received everything from the Lord that He could give. He had given them salvation, the Holy Spirit, the hope of heaven, security, the truth of sound doctrine, spiritual gifts, leaders, abilities, teachers, and gracious blessings. But in spite of it all, they were selfish and loveless. They were self-indulgent and self-centered—wounding each other with their arrogant displays. Spiritual gifts were designed to be used to minister to others, but the Corinthians were using them as a selfish, arrogant, egotistic display. So between two chapters on spiritual gifts (12 and 14) comes this great, great chapter describing love, written by the Holy Spirit to show them that without love all their ministries are nothing but noise—worthless.

II. The Perfections of Love (vv. 4-7)

Before we review the characteristics of love that we have already discussed, I want to review three things that must be understood before verses 4-7 can be understood. First, love can only be described by observing it in action. That's why all the terms in this passage describing love are verbs, not adjectives. Love is not just something you define, it is something you do. Second, love is not a feeling or an attitude; it is an action. Third, love is always related to somebody else, never to self.

In these verses, Paul splits love into all of its components—fifteen qualities. It's as if the great light of God's love hits the prism of Scripture and shatters it into all of the various colors. We have already studied several of these qualities:

A. Love Is Patient (v. 4a; see pp. 49-51)

B. Love Is Kind (v. 4b; see pp. 51-53)

C. Love Is Not Jealous (v. 4c; see pp. 53-58)

D. Love Is Not Boastful (v. 4d; see pp. 63-65)

E. Love Is Not Conceited (v. 4e; see pp. 65-69)

F. Love Is Not Rude (v. 5a; see pp. 69-71)

G. Love Is Not Selfish (v. 5b; see pp. 71-73)

H. Love Is Not Provoked (v. 5c; see pp. 73-75)

We ended our last lesson by discussing this eighth quality of love. Verse 5 tells us that love "is not easily provoked." The word "provoked" literally means "irritated, upset, or angry." So love never gets irritated, upset, or angry.

1. Spiritual anger (see pp. 73-74)

The word translated "provoked" in verse 5 (Gk., *paroxunō*) can also be used in a good sense to refer to righteous indignation. For example, in Acts 17:16 it says, "Now while Paul waited for them at Athens, his spirit was stirred in him, when he saw the city wholly given to idolatry." When it says that Paul's "spirit was stirred," the same Greek word (*paroxunō*) is used. Paul was upset, he was irritated, and he was angry about idolatry. That's righteous indignation! He was angry because something was an affront to God.

2. Self-centered anger (see pp. 74-75)

Paul is not talking about righteous indignation in 1 Corinthians 13:5. He is saying, "Love never gets angry when somebody offends you." He's not talking about God's character being brought into ill repute, or defending the righteous nature of

God; he's simply talking about personal relationships. Love doesn't get irritated, upset, or angry when it is offended by another person.

William Barclay said, "There are in this world only two kinds of people: those who are continually thinking of their rights and those who are continually thinking of their duties." Our duty is to love.

Lesson

a) The defense of personal rights

If you have a problem with getting irritated, upset, and angry—getting mad and losing your temper—it's because you have a mind-set that is selfish. In other words, your whole preoccupation is self-centered. For example, what happens when you're driving down the road and someone cuts you off—squeezing into the little space between you and the car in front of you? What is your reaction? If you get angry, do you know why? Because you wanted that territory you were driving in. Your attitude was, "That's mine!" and somebody took away your rights. You got mad because you had a preset mind to determine that you are the one who matters. It doesn't matter that the person who cut in front of you had to go somewhere, too, and that what he did was a possible option that he had.

The same type of self-centered response is easily seen when two lanes of traffic merge into one. Have you ever noticed that people aren't willing to let you move over into their lane in front of them? They stay one inch off the bumper of the car in front of them just so you can't change lanes. After all, it's their space! Well, how do you handle that? Do you mind, or do you find yourself getting angry? How you respond indicates whether your mind-set is selfish or selfless. It's that simple.

Now, if you get angry, upset, and irritated and then blame it on your circumstances, you're deceiving yourself. The problem isn't your circumstances, it's the preoccupation of your mind that you're important, that your rights matter, that your territory is invincible. When somebody steps into your territory or violates your rights, they trigger that anger because you've already predetermined that you have those rights. In the Corinthian church, for example, if you did something to offend a Christian brother, you could end up in court being sued by him (1 Cor. 6:1-8). The Corinthians were busy defending their rights.

b) The duty to practice love

If you consider everything your duty and nothing your right, you'll never have a problem with anger. If people offend you again and again, your only response will be, "Since my duty is to love them, this is just another wonderful opportunity." The apostle Paul, for example, was a man who never retaliated. Why? Because he was always busy defending God's righteousness. He never cursed the people who stoned him. He never got mad at people who got in his way when he was trying to preach a sermon. He never lambasted the people who threw him in jail. He never said nasty things about the Jewish people who finally had him imprisoned. He never cursed the people who chained him in Rome. Why? Because he never saw anybody as violating his personal rights. Rather, he considered everything in view of his duty to love. You see, love bears the injuries suffered at the hands of others without any irritation. Love is so totally selfless that it never gets on the defensive—it never defends itself.

Now I'm not saying that you're to be ridiculously insensitive to offensive behavior. It's normal to be sensitive and to feel some pain. But for that sensitivity to issue in irritation, upset, anger, and uncontrolled conduct is not Christlike. In fact, I believe that one of the number one reasons for mental and physical illness, particularly in our society, is that everybody is fighting for their own rights instead of looking for the privileged opportunity to perform duties of love.

So Paul isn't saying that we aren't to get provoked about some things. Christians better get provoked about that which offends God, or they'll never do anything significant against the devil. But at the same time, there's no sense in getting mad at each other. To be angry and out of control because of what people do or say about you poisons love. Granville Walker said, "Love is the only cure for irritability; for irritability is only another manifestation of self-centeredness. And love that takes a man outside himself and centers the focus of his attention on the well-being of others is its only cure." The sooner we realize that others matter, the less problem we're going to have with what happens to our own rights.

Let's look, now, at Paul's ninth quality of love.

I . Love Thinks No Evil (v. 5d)

"[Love] thinketh no evil."

1. *Logizomai* defined

The word translated "thinketh" (Gk. *logizomai*) is an accountant's word that literally means "to keep a mathematical calculation." It is a word that is used to refer to the writing of something in a bookkeeper's ledger. Now the reason a bookkeeper writes things in a ledger is so that he won't forget them, right? So, what Paul is saying here is, "Love never keeps books on the evil done to it. Love never keeps a running record of everybody's offense. Love never holds others accountable for some wrong, evil, or injury that they have done. Love just forgives and forgets.''

Chrysostom, the early church father, had a beautiful thought on this subject. What he said went something like this: As a spark is quenched when it falls into the sea, an injury that falls upon a loving Christian is just as surely drowned. That's the way it ought to be. Offenses ought to be drowned in the sea of love.

2. *Logizomai* discussed

Now to illustrate what Paul is saying in 1 Corinthians 13:5, we simply need to look at the word *logizomai*. This word is the same verb that is used in the New Testament to speak of the pardoning act of God. So, since God has not kept any books on our sin, we are not to keep any books on the evils of others. In fact, *logizomai* is often translated in the New Testament with the word *imputed*. For example:

a) What is not imputed

(1) Romans 4:8—"Blessed is the man to whom the Lord will not impute sin." In the language of 1 Corinthians 13:5 it would read, "Blessed is the man of whom the Lord keeps no record of evil." People say, "Well, someday when we get to heaven we're going to face the record of our evil." No, there is no record of our evil. The only thing that's written in each one of our books is the fact that we are declared righteous. Then it's closed and put in the file. Why? Because the Lord does not mathematically add up our sin. He does not keep an accounting of sin. That's a great truth. I'm happy about that, aren't you?

(2) 2 Corinthians 5:19*a*—"To wit, that God was in Christ reconciling the world unto himself, not imputing their trespasses unto them." In other words, God does not keep a record of evil on those who come to Christ. God doesn't keep an accounting nor does He think evil of them. It's a great reality to realize that God never accounts evil to a believer.

You say, "Well, what is on the ledger?"

b) What is imputed

(1) Romans 4:6—"Even as David also describeth the blessedness of the man unto whom God imputeth righteousness apart from works."

(2) Romans 4:22—"And therefore it was imputed to him for righteousness."

(3) James 2:23*a*—"And the scripture was fulfilled which

84

saith, Abraham believed God, and it was imputed unto him for righteousness." In other words, God only keeps account of righteousness, never evil.

Have you ever offended God as a Christian? I have. In fact, I do it all the time. But do you know what? Even though I offend God, He doesn't say, "I'm getting sick of that MacArthur! I'm going to start writing his sins down if he doesn't shape up." He doesn't say that, because He keeps no account. He gives us absolute forgiveness because He loves us, right? God so loves us that He doesn't keep account of our sin; He just forgives it all and keeps on forgiving, and keeps on forgiving, and keeps on forgiving. Resentment, however, keeps the books on other's offenses.

Reminders of Hate

Oftentimes we keep the books on other's offenses. We brood over the record—reading and rereading it—so that the molehill of somebody's offense turns into a mountain of hostility. I've read that in some of the Polynesian Islands, where the natives spend a lot of their time warring and fighting, it is customary for every man to keep visible reminders of his hatred. They do this by suspending little articles from the roof of their huts—with each article representing something about somebody that they hate. You say, "That's incredible! Can you imagine that in our own society? Can you imagine everybody's house decorated like that?" Well, it's not untrue to say that most of our minds have some of those articles of hate hanging in them. That's not something we'd like to admit, but I'm afraid it's true.

Love never makes memories out of evils. Love fast forgets and sees past a person's sin to his potential—the fact that God loves him. Love hesitates to believe any rumor. Love always forgives. Love never keeps account of wrong, never gets irritated, and is never resentful. Do you love like that? Well, that's the way Jesus loved, and that's the way we're to love, too.

J. Love Does Not Rejoice in Unrighteousness (v. 6a)

"[Love] rejoiceth not in iniquity."

The word "iniquity" simply means "unrighteousness." It is the word that talks about sin. Love never rejoices in sin.

1. The ways to rejoice in sin

   a) Rejoicing in your own sin

   There are many, many different ways that people rejoice in sin. Some people rejoice in their own sin and think they're getting away with it. Have you ever heard people brag about sin? They say, "Boy, you know what I did? I did this, and this, and this." That's one way to rejoice in iniquity—just brag about your sin. You say, "Well, certainly Christians would never do that." Oh, really? The Corinthians did. Read 1 Corinthians 5:1-6. Incest was being committed in their midst, and they were proud of it. According to verse 2, they were boasting about it.

Are There Consequences for Sin?

Eternity magazine had an article about Ernest Hemingway a few years ago. It referred to another article in which he had said that people can sin and get away with it. He also said that the old idea of the prudishness of sin, and the Victorian, fundamentalist's viewpoint that there are consequences of sin, was a bunch of baloney. The original article went on to say that Hemingway was living proof of the fact that you can sin and get away with it. Ironically, ten years later to the very day that the article was written, Hemingway took a gun and blew his brains out. He rejoiced over sin only so long.

There are many people who think that the thing to do is to rejoice in their sin. They think it proves their masculinity or gives them a certain invincibility. They see themselves as bigger than God. Now that's one way to rejoice in sin. But there's another way.

b) Rejoicing in somebody else's sin

People rejoice over somebody else's iniquity because it makes them feel quasi-holy. In other words, it justifies their own sin if someone else is sinning—especially if the other person's sin is more obvious. For example:

(1) The salability of newspapers

The salability of newspapers is predicated on the recounting of iniquity, right? The local newspapers would be more appropriately named, the *Los Angeles Unrighteousness* and the *Herald Iniquity*. When you open up the newspaper, what do you read about? So-and-so left his wife, so-and-so was raped, so-and-so committed a crime, so-and-so was murdered, there's corruption over here and corruption over there, and so on. How do we respond to all of that? Unfortunately, we have a tendency to say, "Tsk, tsk, tsk. There they go again," while we gloat in our sanctimonious shell. What we're really doing is trying to convince ourselves that we're holy because we don't do those things. And the fact that somebody does do those things gives us a standard to compare ourselves to. That's rejoicing in iniquity.

(2) The search for legitimate grounds

I've known Christians who have divorced without scriptural grounds. Oftentimes, one partner will eventually realize, after studying the Bible, that the only biblical grounds for the divorce would be fornication. But since there wasn't any, they are not biblically free to remarry. That partner then begins to hope that the other person will commit adultery. That happens more times than I'd like to talk about. People will say to me, "Well, I don't know for sure if they've committed adultery, but I think they have." Then, when they're sure of it, they call me on the phone and excitedly say, "Listen, I just found out that he's committing adultery. I'm free now, right?" It's almost as if they've been praying, "Lord, help him to commit adultery." You say, "Has that really happened?" Yes, I've seen it happen many times. I've seen people get a down-deep wish that their partner would commit adultery, just so they'd have legitimate grounds to remarry. That's rejoicing in the iniquity of someone else, isn't it?

You can rejoice over evil by wishing someone would sin, or by being glad someone does so you look better, or by just enjoying the fact that you sense a certain invincibility when you sin. I've even heard Christians say to me, "I've been committing that sin for a long time, and God hasn't done anything about it yet." Well, God's wheels grind slow, but they grind small!

2. The wrongness of rejoicing in sin

You can't rejoice in iniquity if you love. Do you know why?

a) How it affronts God

Since iniquity affronts God, you won't want to sin. Why? Because if you love God, you won't want Him to be affronted, right? What do you think David means in Psalm 69:9*b* when he says, "The reproaches of those who reproached thee are fallen upon me"? He means, "When You're dishonored, God, I'm in agony." And so you can't rejoice in sin that affronts God.

Look around at what our society does for entertainment, and notice the amount of sin that is tolerated. In fact, our society flaunts outright, overt sin. Now a Christian who rejoices in that sin, or even tolerates it, doesn't understand what it means to love God. Sin is so offensive to the holiness and purity of God, that if you really love God, the sin of others will make you feel cold inside. There certainly would be no place for rejoicing.

So someone who loves God doesn't rejoice in iniquity because it affronts God. Second, there's no thought of rejoicing over evil because of:

b) How it affects sinners

How could you rejoice over someone's sin when you know

the consequences their sin is going to bring? In the same way that sin grieves the heart that loves God, it grieves the heart that loves the sinner—thinking only of how that sinner will suffer chastening and judgment.

The Love of Church Discipline

Christians are never to rejoice in the sin of someone else—especially another Christian. That's why believers are so anxious to correct sin. People say, "Well, if you love everybody, why do you exercise church discipline?" Because loving them is hating their sinfulness. Let me show you an illustration of this in 2 Thessalonians 3. Verse 5a gives us the context. Paul says, "And the Lord direct your hearts into the love of God." In other words, Paul is saying, "I want you to be characterized by love." Then Paul shows us love in action. "Now we command you, brethren, in the name of our Lord Jesus Christ, that ye withdraw yourselves from every brother that walketh disorderly and not after the tradition which he received of us. . . . And if any man obey not our word by this epistle, note that man, and have no company with him, that he may be ashamed. Yet count him not as an enemy, but admonish him as a brother" (vv. 6, 14-15).

In other words, Paul says, "If a believer persists in sin and won't turn from it, you're to put him out of the church. You're to cut your fellowship off and not have anything to do with him." Why? Because that's part of letting the love of God control your life. Since love hates sin, it goes to the sinner and says, "That isn't right." Love also purifies the fellowship and removes the sin that might taint the remainder of the people. So when somebody comes along and says, "Your church disciplines? Don't you think that's less than loving?" I say, "No. That is loving." You see, love doesn't tolerate evil. Love doesn't rejoice in sin. Why? Because sin affronts God, and it brings punishment on the sinner.

3. The wagging tongue that rejoices in sin

First Corinthians 13:6a also includes the issue of gossip, because love doesn't recount evil things. I have often wondered how much of our conversation would be silenced if we never gossiped about the faults and sins of others. What would we do? If we didn't read the paper about all the evil that is happening around the world, and if we didn't talk about the failures, faults, and sins of the people around us, what would we talk about? This subject is often missed in discussions of 1 Corinthians 13:6, yet this passage, next to James 3, is probably the most stringent indictment in the New Testament against gossiping. Love "rejoiceth not in iniquity." And if it doesn't rejoice in it, it isn't happy to hear it or to pass it on. Some people say, "I'm just telling the truth. I know this to be a fact." Well, that doesn't mean you have to say it.

There's a teaching going around today called sensitivity training that says, "Tell everybody the truth, be completely open and transparent, and never be afraid to spill your guts—regardless of how it will affect someone else." Well, since love doesn't rejoice in somebody's evil, it doesn't go passing it around either. Why would you pass around something that affronts God? Why would you pass around something that wounds and injures the sinner who did it? If you were loving to God and loving to that individual, you wouldn't.

The Whole Truth and Nothing but the Truth

There was a country newspaper editor who got tired of people who were always writing to the paper and saying, "You don't report the news with enough honesty. You're too biased, and you're always too kind." He decided to respond to such complaints and announced that in the next issue he would tell the whole truth about everybody and everything. Well, the people were so eager to get the paper, it sold out immediately. Let me share with you three sample articles that were in this paper:

"Dave Conkey died at his home last Friday evening, and there was a big funeral Sunday afternoon. The minister said it was a loss to the community, but I doubt it. The community is better off without him. The doctor said he died of a heart attack. Nonsense! Whiskey killed him."

Another article: "The Wednesday Literary Club met at the home of Mrs. Gadabout. The program stated they were going to study Shakespeare's play *Much Ado About Nothing*. Well, they didn't. The lady who was assigned to present the paper had never read the play, and so they had no program. But they made up for it by gossiping about every member that wasn't there, and the whole afternoon was really like the play—much ado about nothing."

Another article went like this: "Winnifred Jones and Jim Smith were married Saturday at the Methodist Parsonage. The bride is a very ordinary girl who doesn't know any more about cooking than a jackrabbit and never helped her mother three days in her whole life. She is not a beauty by any means and has a gait like a duck. The groom is an up-to-date loafer. He spends most of his time hanging around the pool hall. He has been living off his old folks at home all his life and is not worth shucks. It will be a hard life for both of them." Well, so much for the paper.

The following letter was written by a woman who had decided

not to lie when asked to give a recommendation for someone who had worked for her. This was her recommendation: "The bearer of this letter was in our employ for one month. We engaged her to do light housework and she couldn't have done it any lighter. We found her extremely careful to break only our best dishes and glassware. She was neat about the house, always hiding the sweepings under the rug where they would not be seen. In serving meals she exhibited good training by never putting her thumb in the soup when it was too hot and never spilled it except on our company. Her cooking was exceptional; in fact, we took daily exception to it. We shall always gratefully remember her stay with us; it was so short." Well, there's something to be said for a little veiled honesty, isn't there?

You see, love isn't looking to parade everybody's evil. Love doesn't laugh and make scorn. Love hides those kinds of things gently. Love rejoices not in iniquity. I like the definition of gossip that says this: "Gossip is vice enjoyed vicariously." But love doesn't do that. Love hates the sin, the way it hurts God, and the way it hurts the sinner.

Granville Walker said, "There are times when silence is yellow. . . . times when we ought to stand on our feet, and regardless of the consequences, challenge the gross evils of the time; and times when not to do so is the most blatant form of cowardice. But there are other times when silence is golden, when to tell the truth is to make many hearts bleed needlessly and when nothing is accomplished and everything is hurt by a loose tongue." He's right, isn't he?

Love never rejoices in iniquity. It never rejoices in what offends God or in what harms the sinner. Therefore, it never likes to hear it or pass it on.

You say, "Well, what *does* love rejoice in?" The end of verse 6 tells us and gives us the eleventh characteristic of love.

K. Love Rejoices with the Truth (v. 6*b*)

"[Love] rejoiceth in [lit. "with"] the truth."

Love doesn't rejoice in unrighteousness, it rejoices with the truth. Now that's an interesting comparison. Why does Paul compare those two? Why doesn't he say, "Love rejoices with righteousness"? Because it is clear that righteousness is predicated on truth. You can't be righteous until you behave yourself in accord with God's truth.

1. Its basis

   a) Identified

   There are two things I want you to see: Love only rejoices with truth as it is taught and as it is lived. Love can't rejoice with error or false teaching. Love can't tolerate wrong doctrine. Yet you hear people say today, "Well, we don't want to make an issue out of what they believe. We just want to love them." This is the attitude behind what is commonly known as the "Ecumenical Movement." This kind of thinking has stimulated all kinds of people to get together under the name of love.

I talked to a well-known Christian leader, and I asked him, "How can you compromise yourself with people who do not believe the Word of God in the way we know it to be true?" "Well," he said, "we are instructed in the Word of God to love them." My answer to that is this: "Love rejoices with the truth." That is the only basis on which love can work. I can't put my arms around and love somebody who teaches things other than what the Bible teaches, nor can I put my arms around and love somebody, in the truest sense, who lives a life that does not behave itself according to the truth.

Love will rejoice when truth is taught and when truth is lived. It will not rejoice when those are absent. And believe me, the slightest compromise will take the joy out of love. I may love you, but when you teach error or when you live error, I will not rejoice. The slightest compromise robs that joy.

b) Illustrated

In 2 John, we find a very helpful illustration of this. Beginning in verse 6 it says, "And this is love, that we walk after his commandments." What does John say love is? Well, it's not a feeling or an attitude. It's obedience to the truth. Verse 6 continues, "This is the commandment, that, as ye have heard from the beginning, ye should walk in it." Love is obedience and living in the truth. Love doesn't disregard the truth and say, "Oh well, it doesn't matter what you believe or how you live; I love you anyway." No! Love walks after the commandments.

You say, "Well, what if somebody varies just a little bit in their doctrine?" Verse 7 moves right into that. "For many deceivers are entered into the world, who confess not that Jesus Christ cometh in the flesh." In other words, they throw doubts on the incarnation in some way or another. "This is a deceiver and an antichrist. Look to yourselves, that [you] lose not those things which [you] have wrought, but that [you] receive a full reward" (v. 8). He's saying that we can lose our reward by fooling around with such people.

Continuing on, John says, "Whosoever transgresseth, and abideth not in the doctrine of Christ, hath not God. . . . If there come any unto you, and bring not this doctrine, receive him not into your house, neither bid him Godspeed; for he that biddeth him Godspeed is partaker of his evil deeds" (vv. 9*a*, 10-11).

John's just talking about love here, but he's saying that love is no excuse for indiscriminate behavior in regard to truth. Do you see? Love operates in the area of the commandments, and love responds toward the people who teach the truth. So, love rejoices in those who teach the truth and with those who live the truth. But love doesn't rejoice indiscriminately with anybody and anything who just happen to throw the name God or Jesus around. The Bible, you see, is very stern in dealing with sin in behavior and with sin in doctrine.

Let's look, now, at the positive aspect of rejoicing with the truth.

2. Its benefits

Do you know what love does? Instead of parading somebody's evil, love finds the good in people and talks about that. I love to be around people like that, don't you? They help me so much. I call that kind of person a "plus" person. A "minus" person is somebody who goes around subtracting from people's reputations. I want to be a plus person. I want to add to people instead of subtracting from them.

You say, "But what if there isn't something good in a certain individual to talk about?" There's always something good! If Jesus could see some potential in Peter, He was definitely a plus person. Most of us would have fired Peter at the beginning of his ministry, but Jesus didn't. Jesus could see a plus in the life of a harlot who washed His feet with penitent tears, when the Pharisee could see nothing but a minus. Jesus could see a plus in a half-breed Samaritan. Jesus was a plus person. He added to people; He didn't subtract from people. Love is a plus—it's positive. It encourages goodness, finds the best in a person, and then exalts it.

I hope you teach your children to be plus people. I hope they grow up learning to say good things about others. You'll find that children will bloom in the sunshine of the spirit that encourages, helps, and builds them up.

There was a dear Scottish minister who all his life loved the simple people in Scotland. When he died, someone said of him, "Now there is no one left in our village to appreciate the triumphs of ordinary folks." I hope there's somebody in your family to appreciate the triumphs of ordinary folks. Love does, you know. It looks for the truth and the true behavior and then rejoices with it. And by rejoicing when there's good behavior, it encourages more good behavior. But if all you ever do is depreciate others, that's the kind of response you'll get. If people find that you are lifting them up when truth exists, then they'll want and seek the truth. Love always rejoices in the truth.

Let's sum up what we've discussed in this lesson. Love is so selfless that it never gets irritated or upset; it is so concerned about the welfare of somebody else that it never keeps books on any evil done to it; it is so zealous for the holiness of God and the health of a person that it never rejoices in unrighteousness; and since the standard of joy is always the truth, it rejoices when the truth is taught and lived. Love is not for the halfhearted, the sentimental, or the weakling. To live by love is one of the most difficult things there is. It takes the most strength, the most discipline, and the most commitment, and the most faith of anything I've ever discovered in the Bible. But without it we're nothing!

Focusing on the Facts

1. What three facts about love must be understood before the specific qualities of love in 1 Corinthians 13:4-7 can be properly understood (see p. 81)?

2. How is Paul described in Acts 17:16? What was he reacting to? What caused him to respond that way? According to the characteristic of love in 1 Corinthians 13:5, was Paul loving the Athenians? Explain (see p. 81).

3. As Christians, should we be thinking more about our rights or our duties? What is produced in our lives when we concentrate on our rights? What's produced when we concentrate on our duties (see pp. 82-83)?

4. In one word, what is the Christian's duty to others? How did Paul exemplify that in his own life (see p. 83)?

5. At the end of 1 Corinthians 13:5, Paul says that love "thinketh no evil." How does the definition of the Greek word for "thinketh" (*logizomai*) clarify this quality of divine love (see pp. 83-84)?

6. The Greek word (*logizomai*) is used throughout the New Testament to speak of what important act of God? What English word is *logizomai* often translated into (see p. 84)?

7. According to Romans 4:8 and 2 Corinthians 5:19, does God keep a record of the sins of believers? What word in these verses refers to God's record keeping (see pp. 84-85)?

8. In regard to sin, what is written on the ledger of every Christian (see pp. 84-85)?

9. What are some synonyms for the word "iniquity" in 1 Corinthians 13:6 (see p. 85)?

10. What are the two basic ways that people rejoice in sin? Which is the most common for Christians? Why (see pp. 85-86)?

11. What are some examples of the different ways that Christians rejoice in sombody else's iniquity (see pp. 86-87)?

12. A Christian who is characterized by the divine love of God can't rejoice in iniquity for two major reasons. What are they (see pp. 87-88)?

13. What's wrong with the view that sees church discipline as an unloving practice (see p. 88)?

14. Apart from James 3, what passage in the New Testament is the most stringent indictment against gossiping (see p. 88)?

15. As Christians, we are to be truthful (Eph. 4:15*a*, 25). How does that relate to the "truthfulness" of sensitivity training, which advocates saying whatever you are thinking, regardless of how it will affect someone else (see p. 89)?

16. Love rejoices with truth as it is _____ and as it is _____ (see p. 90).

17. What is wrong with the following statement: "Everybody needs to put aside their doctrinal differences and love one another" (see p. 91)?

18. According to 2 John 6-11, how does love respond to someone who doesn't walk according to the truth or to someone who doesn't teach the truth (see pp. 91-92)?

19. Define what it means to be a "plus" person. What does it mean to be a "minus" person? How would you classify Jesus in this regard? Give some examples to back up your answer (see p. 92).

Pondering the Principles

1. If you have a problem getting irritated, upset, and angry with people, it's probably because you have a preoccupation with yourself and a mind-set that you will always defend your own personal rights. The illustration given in this lesson made reference to the irritation that people experience when they drive their car (see p. 82). You may not have a problem in that area, but there is probably at least one area in which you find yourself getting more irritated than in others. Evaluate what it is that gets you upset. Can it be boiled down to a defense of your personal rights? What perspective should you have if you are to have victory over the problem of getting mad and losing your temper? If you really want to change, ask God to bring circumstances into your life that will give you the opportunity to act in love toward those that offend you—to see the duty to love as more important than the defense of your rights.

2. Have you ever said, "I forgive you," to somebody but brought up their offense at a later time—either directly to them or in your mind? Can you truly forgive someone without also forgetting their offense? Is there someone that you really don't like being around anymore because they offended you in the past? If so, you're still keeping an account of their sin against you, right? Recognize your lack of forgiveness as sin and confess it to the Lord. Thank God for the fact that he doesn't keep an account of your sins (see Ps. 103:12; Isa. 44:22; Mic. 7:18-19), then meditate on Matthew 18:21-35.

3. When you see a fellow Christian sin, how are you to respond? Read Matthew 18:15-17, and write down the steps for dealing with a sinning

brother. How are these steps related to 1 Peter 4:8? Are you often tempted to talk about someone else's sin? After love deals with a person's sin, it covers it with silence. Love certainly doesn't gossip about it. How much of your conversation would be silenced if you never gossiped about the faults and sins of others? At the end of each day, try and recall how often you gossiped about someone else's faults. Confess it, and then commit yourself to love the brethren by not rejoicing in their sin or repeating it to others.

4. Instead of talking about the faults of people, love finds the good in them and talks about that instead. When you hear someone say negative things about another person, make an effort to say something positive about them. Oftentimes, you'll find that negative people will become silent when their negative comments fall on positive ears. How do your children hear you talk about others? Do they hear you gossip and say negative things, or do they hear you say good things? Teach your children to see the good in people by first doing it yourself.

6
The Qualities of True Love—
Part 4

Outline

Introduction
A. The Effects of Sin
    1. Spiritual
    2. Physical
        a) Illustrated
        b) Investigated
            (1) The source of physiological problems
            (2) The specifics of physiological problems
B. The Example of Sin
C. The Elimination of Sin
    1. The importance of love
        a) Matthew 22:34-40
        b) Romans 13:8-10
        c) 1 Timothy 1:5*a*
        d) 1 Corinthians 16:14
    2. The injunctions to love

Review
  I. The Prominence of Love
 II. The Perfections of Love
    A. Love Is Patient
    B. Love Is Kind
    C. Love Is Not Jealous
    D. Love Is Not Boastful
    E. Love Is Not Conceited
    F. Love Is Not Rude
    G. Love Is Not Selfish
    H. Love Is Not Provoked
    I. Love Thinks No Evil
    J. Love Does Not Rejoice in Unrighteousness
    K. Love Rejoices with the Truth

Lesson
    L. Love Bears All Things
        1. The word defined

2. The word discussed
   a) The redirected character of love
     (1) Our natural response
     (2) Our new response
       (*a*) 1 Peter 4:8*b*
       (*b*) Proverbs 10:12
   b) The redemptive character of love
     (1) Suppressing someone's sin
     (2) Sympathizing with someone's sin
     (3) Suffering for someone's sin

M. Love Believes All Things
  1. Believing the best
   a) About an unbelieving child
   b) About an unbelieving spouse
   c) About sinful disciples
  2. Believing the worst
   a) About Job
   b) About Jesus

N. Love Hopes All Things
  1. Hope's object
  2. Hope's optimism
  3. Hope's obstacle

O. Love Endures All Things
  1. The term explained
  2. The term exemplified
   a) The apostle Stephen
   b) The Lord Jesus

Conclusion
A. The Fact of Love's Importance
B. The Five Keys to Love's Implementation

Introduction

A. The Effects of Sin

Sin has effects. I doubt whether any of us would even bother to argue that it doesn't. We know that it does. We know that it has effects by virtue of our understanding of Scripture and our understanding of our own circumstances. We recognize that when sin is in our lives, there are certain things that take place as a result. And we recognize that the Bible talks about the consequences of sin.

I suppose we could divide the effects of sin into two obvious categories.

1. Spiritual

First of all, sin has a great effect on the soul of a man or woman. It affects your relationship with God. When you sin, or live in a state of unconfessed sin, you forfeit blessing, you take yourself out of the place of being blessed by God, and you put yourself in a place where there is no joy. There's a soul sickness that occurs—a languishing of the soul—when a believer is sinful.

2. Physical

Sin will have results in pain and illness. A good illustration of that is David.

a) Illustrated

In 2 Samuel 12 we have the record of a rather terrible sin. David violated Bathsheba, and then as a secondary act, he ordered for her husband to be killed in battle, which was the equivalent of murder. So David was involved in adultery and murder. And as a result of sin, he not only suffered spiritually—the soul sickness that came, the terrible blight on his soul, the sense of alienation from God, and the anxiety of that sin as he realized he had forfeited the place of blessing—but there also came a rather dramatic impact on his own physical body.

Let's look for a moment at Psalm 32 and see how David reacted to the physical illness that came upon him as a result of his sin. In Psalm 32, David is talking about his sin and how wonderful it would be if he could get out from under it. Notice that the effects of his sin, in verses 3 and 4, are in the physical area. He says, "When I kept silence [i.e., when I failed to acknowledge my sin, confess it, and deal with it before God], my bones became old through my roaring all the day long." Here we see that David actually had physical pain. The physical consequence of his sin was an aching of his bones—a deep-down physical pain. Then in verse 4 David says, "For day and night thy hand was heavy upon me; my moisture is turned into the drought of summer." David's life juices dried up. Things happened to his blood and to the secretion of various glands in his body. The fluids that accommodate the muscles were perhaps not operating properly—possibly causing tention in his muscles. That's the Hebrew significance of the word "moisture." So David's situation is a vivid example of the tremendous physical impact that sin can have.

b) Investigated

(1) The source of physiological problems

For a Christian, sin constitutes emotional trauma. No question about it. It creates emotional anxiety and emotional alienation from the only anchor that the Christian has. As a result of that emotional trauma, a debilitating or even fatal illness can occur. The emotional center of the brain is a stem from which nerve fibers run to every organ in the body. And because of such an intricate connection to the brain, turmoil in the emotional center of the brain can create impulses that can cause any number of physiological problems.

(2) The specifics of physiological problems

Physicians tell us that physiological problems due to emotional anxiety are created along three lines:

(*a*) The emotional center in the brain causes a change in the amount of blood flow to a given organ. This can become debilitating to that organ.

(*b*) Emotional trauma can create an effect on the secretion of certain glands, which also can affect bodily function.

(*c*) Emotional trauma can also affect the change in tension of certain muscles.

B. The Example of Sin

When Paul wrote to the Corinthians to tell them that they needed to love, it wasn't just for the healing of their souls; it no doubt had great consequences for their bodies, as well. Let me show you why I say that. Look back at chapter 11 of 1 Corinthians. In verse 29, in reference to the sinful way in which they were partaking of the Lord's Table, Paul says, "For he that eateth and drinketh unworthily, eateth and drinketh judgment [or "chastening"] to himself, not discerning the Lord's body." In other words, "If you eat this way, you're going to get chastened." Verse 30 continues, "For this cause many are weak and sickly among you, and many sleep." They had had sickness, severe illness, and even death.

Now, I don't think the idea here is that God gave them a supernatural illness or miraculously killed them. That may happen (see Acts 5:1-11), but more likely what happened here is that people in the Corinthian assembly were living in sin and experiencing physical ramifications. So when the apostle Paul in chapter 13 says to them, "Love each other," he is not simply saying, "This is a soul issue," he's saying, "This is a body issue as well. For the wholeness of your assembly and for the wholeness of your own body, you need to love."

C. The Elimination of Sin

Now remember, all sin is a violation of love—all of it! So Paul is simply saying to the Corinthians, "You are sick both spiritually and physically because you are sinning. But if you start loving one another all of these things will disappear." You say, "John, are you saying that love will eliminate all sin?" Yes, I am. Let me show you why.

1. The importance of love

a) Matthew 22:34-40

In verse 34 we read, "But when the Pharisees had heard that

he had put the Sadducees to silence, they were gathered together." The Pharisees were always trying to prove themselves better than the Sadducees. They figured that since the Sadducees had been humiliated by Jesus, if they got the best of Him, they would have the upper hand in their society. So they prompted one particular lawyer to ask Jesus a question. In verse 36 he asks, "Master, which is the great commandment in the law?" Now, even though they believed that they had to keep the law to be saved, they were smart enough to realize that nobody could keep the law. So some of them decided that if they could just find one good law and keep it, they'd be all right. They were simply asking, then, which law was the best one to keep. Jesus answers the lawyer's question in verses 37-40 and introduces the concept of love in relation to the law. "Thou shalt love the Lord, thy God, with all thy heart, and with all thy soul, and with all thy mind. This is the first and great commandment. And the second is like it, Thou shalt love thy neighbor as thyself. On these two commandments hang all the law and the prophets."

Now, if you love the Lord your God with all your heart, soul, mind, and strength, and if you love your neighbor properly as yourself, you will never sin. Why? Because you won't do anything to violate God or your neighbor—that takes care of it. Love, then, fulfills it all.

b) Romans 13:8-10

In Romans 13 Paul says, "Owe no man any thing, but to love one another; for he that loveth another hath fulfilled the law. For this, Thou shalt not commit adultery, Thou shalt not kill, Thou shalt not steal, Thou shalt not bear false witness, Thou shalt not covet; and if there be any other commandment, it is briefly comprehended in this saying, namely, Thou shalt love thy neighbor as thyself. Love worketh no ill to its neighbor; therefore, love is the fulfilling of the law." In other words, you don't need a commandment that says, "Thou shalt not kill your neighbor," if you love your neighbor. You don't need a commandment that says, "Don't covet," if you love the person who possesses what you don't have.

Both of those passages essentially say the same thing. And what they say is this: To simplify all of living, love God and your neighbor—and you won't have to worry about anything else.

c) 1 Timothy 1:5*a*

Paul writes, "Now the end of the commandment [i.e., the reason, the objective, the sum, the point of it all] is love out of a pure heart." God is trying to get us to love.

d) 1 Corinthians 16:14

Paul told the Corinthians, "Let all your things be done with love." Proper theology is no substitute for love. Activism and service can't substitute for love. Selective affection (or attraction to certain people) is no substitute for a widespread love. And immaturity or ignorance can't be used as an excuse not to practice love. In fact, in 1 Thessalonians 4:9, Paul writes to the Thessalonians and says, "But, as touching brotherly love, ye need not that I write unto you; for ye yourselves are taught of God to love one another." Romans 5:5 says that "the love of God is shed abroad in our hearts."

God wants Christians to be happy and healthy in their souls. God wants you to know what it is to be blessed. He doesn't want you to feel His chastening or experience physical illness that comes from the trauma of willful sin. The real key to all of it is to learn to love. This is the indispensable reality for the Christian. God is love. So if God is to be seen in us, it is going to be when we express His love.

2. The injunctions to love

Now, it is so important that we love, that the New Testament just keeps hammering away at it. For example, Christians are exhorted to:

a) Put on love (Col. 3:14)

b) Follow after love (1 Cor. 14:1)

c) Abound in love (Phil. 1:9)

d) Continue in love (Heb. 13:1)

e) Increase in love (1 Thess. 3:12)

f) Be fervent in love (1 Pet. 4:8)

g) Be consistent in love (Phil. 2:2)

h) Provoke each other to love (Heb. 10:24)

i) Be sincere in love (2 Cor. 8:8)

Love has always been the pinnacle of life. It's the pinnacle of wholeness for the Christian. The healthy, happy, positive, glowing, useful Christian is the one who loves. You say, "Oh, that's great, John, but how does it work? How does love function?"

Review

I. The Prominence of Love (vv. 1-3; see pp. 12-21, 29-42)

II. The Perfections of Love (vv. 4-7)

   A. Love Is Patient (v. 4*a*; see pp. 49-51)

   B. Love Is Kind (v. 4*b*; see pp. 51-53)

   C. Love Is Not Jealous (v. 4*c*; see pp. 53-58)

D. Love Is Not Boastful (v. 4*d*; see pp. 63-65)

E. Love Is Not Conceited (v. 4*e*; see pp. 65-69)

F. Love Is Not Rude (v. 5*a*; see pp. 69-71)

G. Love Is Not Selfish (v. 5*b*; see pp. 71-73)

H. Love Is Not Provoked (v. 5*c*; see pp. 73-75, 81-83)

I. Love Thinks No Evil (v. 5*d*; see pp. 83-85)

J. Love Does Not Rejoice in Unrighteousness (v. 6*a*; see pp. 85-90)

K. Love Rejoices with the Truth (v. 6*b*; see pp. 90-93)

Lesson

Let's look at the last four qualities of love in verse 7. "[Love] beareth all things, believeth all things, hopeth all things, endureth all things." These are statements of exaggeration—hyperbole. The phrase "all things," which is used four times in this verse, isn't referring to all things universally. Love certainly has to make some discrimination. First John 4:1*b* says that we have to "try the spirits [to see] whether they are of God." We don't believe the devil, do we? The phrase "all things" doesn't mean all things in the general, total, universal sense. It does mean, however, all things within the limit of proper biblical boundaries and proper Christian discrimination—all things that come into the divine framework.

These four qualities of love are ascending and are probably more closely tied than any of the other eleven. They really go together. Let's look at them.

L. Love Bears All Things (v. 7*a*)

"[Love] beareth all things."

This is a tremendous word—a glorious truth. The word "beareth," although it is used in various shades of meaning in the New Testament, primarily means "to cover with silence" or "to suppress." That's the basic meaning. It doesn't mean that love puts up with anything and gets shoved around because of a lack of dignity. What it means is this: Love, out of regard, respect, and honest concern for the real value of another person, will do everything it can to cover up and suppress the sin of that person. Genuine love is reluctant to drag a scandal in front of anyone. So when Paul says that love "beareth all things," he's not talking about enduring a trial, he's talking about covering the ugliness in someone else's life.

2. The word discussed

   a) The redirected character of love

      (1) Our natural response

         It is normal for depravity to want to uncover everybody's evil. You can illustrate the fact that this is a normal human behavior pattern just by looking at yourself and your own children. There's no question about it. The newsstands are filled with magazines that do nothing more than expose people's sin. And all the bookstores are jammed with exposés. You see, depravity is always looking to find the skeleton in somebody else's closet. Do you know why? Because it gives people a sense of self-righteousness.

Children are a good illustration of this. They come into the world depraved, don't they? And one of the first manifestations of their depravity is the eagerness with which they want to tattle on their brothers and sisters. One of my children will come to me and say, "Do you know what Matt's doing?" (Obviously trying to get him in trouble.) I'll say, "I don't know what Matt's doing, and I'm not interested." Another one of them will come running down the stairs yelling, "So-and-so's jumping on the bed!" Well, that's typical, isn't it? Why? Because depravity is always trying to uncover somebody else so it can gain a sense of self-respect and self-righteousness.

It's sad, but some people never grow out of that. Some people spend their whole lives tattling on others. I always wonder about married people who constantly talk about the errors and the faults and the sins of their partner. I question whether they know the meaning of love, because love throws a blanket over somebody else's faults.

The Corinthians didn't know the meaning of covering sin. They exposed everybody. In chapter 6, we read that if somebody offended one of them, they dragged him into court and sued him publicly before a pagan judge. But love doesn't do that. Love throws a kindly mantle over the faults, weaknesses, and sins of others.

(2) Our new response

    (a) 1 Peter 4:8b—"For love shall cover the multitude of sins." Love is a big blanket that runs around throwing itself over people's faults—not exposing them.

    (b) Proverbs 10:12—"Hatred stirreth up strifes, but love covereth all sins." Have you ever noticed how easily you dismiss the faults of those you love? They do something wrong, and you say, "That's okay. Everybody makes a mistake." But how do you respond when someone you don't like does something wrong? You love it, don't you? Why? Because you want them to do something wrong and look bad. But love dismisses the sins of the one it loves.

Now love will warn, and exhort, and rebuke, and discipline, but love will also cover that sin and not expose it. It's a

103

beautiful characteristic of love.

b) The redemptive character of love

(1) Suppressing someone's sin

The best illustration I can think of to describe the characteristic of love that bears all things is the cross of Jesus Christ. Love has a redemptive quality. God loved us, but He didn't sit up in heaven and say, "You know, those human beings are awful. What do you angels think about them?" They didn't have an internal discussion about us. Isn't it nice to know that we are not the subject of heavenly gossip? Do you know what God did? He said, "Because of their evil, I better take My big blanket and go down and cover their sin." And that's what He did, didn't He? The Bible says that God loved us so much, that He "sent his Son to be the propitiation for our sins" (1 John 4:10*b*). Do you know what the word "propitiation" means? It means "covering." Jesus is the covering for our sin.

You see, God is not in the business of exposing sin, He's in the business of covering it. Rather than sit in righteous resentment and gossip within the Trinity and with the angels about the sins of men, God came to a cross, threw a mantle over their sin, and bore their sins in His own body. Love throws a mantle over sin and suppresses it because it has a redemptive element.

(2) Sympathizing with someone's sin

Isaiah 53 says, "Surely he hath borne our griefs, and carried our sorrows. . . . But he was wounded for our transgressions, he was bruised for our iniquities; the chastisement for our peace was upon him" (vv. 4*a*, 5*a*). Now that is love. Love will actually go beyond throwing a blanket over sin. Love is so sympathetic that it will feel the pain and endure the agony. Love will bear it. When a brother or sister sins, love will feel the pain. If I love that person, I hurt for them. That's why I won't expose their sin to others. Love is willing to bear the pain.

Henry Ward Beecher beautifully said, "God pardons like a mother who kisses the offense into everlasting forgetfulness." That's what God does. The redemptive character of love is willing to throw a blanket over sin and to sympathize with that sin. Third, it also involves:

(3) Suffering for someone's sin

The redemptive character of love is willing to take on the consequence of sin and endure the suffering. On the cross, God didn't just throw a mantle over sin and feel sympathetic about it, He also bore our sins in His own body.

104

Genuine love is never quick to exploit, expose, gloat, or condemn. It throws a blanket over sin, is burdened over it, and even takes the blame and accepts the punishment for it.

The Ring of Death Silenced by Love

In seventeenth-century England during the time of General Cromwell, a soldier was condemned to die by execution at the ringing of the curfew bell. This soldier, however, was engaged to be married to a beautiful young girl. With tears, the girl pleaded with the judge and with Cromwell to spare his young life. But it was all in vain. The preparations were made for the execution, and the city awaited the signal from the bell at curfew. The sexton, who was old and deaf, threw himself against the rope, as he had for years. He pulled it and pulled it and pulled it not realizing that no sound was coming from the bell. The girl had climbed to the top of the belfry, and had reached out, caught, and held on to the tongue of the huge bell at the risk of her life. As the sexton rang it, she was smashed against the sides of the bell—but the bell was silent. At length, the bell ceased to swing, and she managed to descend from the tower, wounded and bleeding. Cromwell, waiting at the place of execution, wanted to know why the bell had not rung. The girl arrived and told him what she had done. A poet recorded it for all time. This is what he said:

> At his feet she told her story,
> Showed her hands all bruised and torn;
> And her sweet young face, still haggard
> With the anguish it had worn;
> Touched his heart with sudden pity,
> Lit his eyes with misty light:
> "Go, your lover lives," said Cromwell,
> "Curfew will not ring tonight."

Now, that's somebody who was willing to go where love goes—to throw a mantle over sin, to feel sympathy for sin, and to take the punishment for sin—somebody else's sin. That's redemptive love.

Love that bears all things suppresses someone else's sin, sympathizes with someone else's sin, and suffers for someone else's sin—if it can. To what extent do you bear the pain to cover someone's sin? Do you really cover other people's evil? Love does. Love bears all things.

M. Love Believes All Things (v. 7*b*)

"[Love] believeth all things."

Love believes the best in someone else. Instead of being suspicious and eager to denounce an offender, love believes the best. Instead of saying, "He probably got exactly what he deserved" or "He's so far gone now, he'll probably never change," love believes the best. Love sees the weakness, throws a mantle of silence over it, and then believes the best. Love doesn't go through life cynical and suspicious—suspecting everybody and everything. Love doesn't automatically jump to the conclusion that when somebody does something wrong it proves that they were rotten to begin with. Love always believes the best.

1. Believing the best

   a) About an unbelieving child

   The characteristic of love that believes the best about someone is often seen in the hearts of parents who have a child that drifts away from the Lord. I met a couple at a conference recently who have a daughter that drifted away from the Lord. She is a source of great heartbreak to them. Now even though they recognize her sins, her faults, and her problems, they have thrown a mantle of love over her. And they believe with all their hearts that she'll come back to the Lord. Do you know why they believe that? Because they love her—and love has to believe that. Love cares too much not to believe it. When love wants something badly enough, it turns into faith. That mom and dad want that girl back so badly, and they love her so much, that their wish has become a belief. But that's what love does. Now, if they had responded by saying, "She's lost forever. She'll never come back to the Lord!" it would reveal that they don't love her. Why? Because love doesn't let go like that.

   b) About an unbelieving spouse

   I know a Christian woman who has been married to an unbelieving husband for thirty years. Yet she's always saying, "He'll come to Christ someday." Do you know what that tells me? That tells me that she loves him. Her love for him makes her wish that he'd become a Christian, and that wish becomes so strong, it turns into a belief that he will. Yes, love sees wrong and weakness, and love rebukes it and deals with it. But love does not seek to expose it; it throws a mantle over it.

   This is also illustrated by Jesus in the way that He believed the best:

   c) About sinful disciples

   Just think about Jesus and His disciples. They weren't anything special, quite frankly. The ones that are the most well known in the New Testament—Peter, James, and John— were sinful, weren't they? Peter, who was notorious for his faithlessness, continually fell on his face. James and John had a problem with pride and pseudospirituality. They had the gall to ask their mother to ask Jesus if they could have the chief seats in the kingdom. Now we don't know very much about the rest of the disciples, but we do know that they were sinners, too.

Now, Jesus could have scratched His head and said, "Father, I don't know what to tell You, but I don't think this plan is going to work out. I have twelve losers for disciples. If You think I ought to come back to heaven and turn everything over to them, I'll do it—but it's a little risky." Jesus didn't say that, though, did He? Jesus knew the sins of the disciples better than anyone else, yet He believed the best about every one of them. He said, "They can do it," gave them the task, and sent them into the world. And they succeeded, didn't they? In fact, do you know what I think? I tend to think you make the best out of the people you believe the most in. Jesus believed the best about them and trusted them to fulfill His plan. And on that basis they carried it out.

Err of the Side of Love

If you're going to make a mistake about somebody's character, do yourself a favor and err on the side of love. Make a mistake in the fact that you trusted and believed in them too much. Now, if somebody doesn't fulfill that trust once in a while, it's all right. It's better to err on the side of love. You'll find that most of the time it will put the kind of positive influence on people that will make them want to give the best they have.

2. Believing the worst

The Corinthians were suspecting and cynical, anxious to believe the worst about people, and assumed that nobody ever told the truth. This is also seen in the "friends" that believed the worst:

a) About Job

Job's friends were quick to accuse, weren't they? "We know what your problem is, Job—you're evil. You're a bad egg, Job. Face it! That's why you're having all these problems." Well, Job listened to all of that palaver about as long as anybody could. He knew in his own heart, however, that his friends were wrong. Finally, in Job 21:27, Job says, "Behold, I know your thoughts, and the devices which ye wrongfully imagine against me." In other words, "I've had it with you guys. All you do is think evil about me." And that just proved that they didn't love him. If they had loved him they'd have said, "Job's a good man. Maybe he's made mistakes here and there, and maybe he's sinned, but he's a

107

good man. There's something redeemable about him." But that's not the way they thought.

Another illustration of this is the Pharisees, who were, constantly believing the worst:

b) About Jesus

Do you want to know how the Pharisees felt about Jesus? Matthew 9 gives you as clear an indication as you'll ever get. Jesus had met a man sick of the palsy. And because He saw that this man and his friends had great faith, Jesus said, "Son, be of good cheer; thy sins be forgiven thee" (v. 2b). Jesus gave him salvation and then later gave him physical healing as well (v. 7).

After Jesus forgave this man of his sins, verse 3 says, "And, behold, certain of the scribes said within themselves, This man blasphemeth." Now this is interesting. Jesus says, "Your sins be forgiven," and the Pharisees say within themselves (not out loud), "This man blasphemes." Now, why did they say that? I believe it's because they had a predetermination that He was evil. You say, "Is it evil to forgive sins?" No, of course not! But they had a predisposition that He was evil, so whatever He did had to be evil. They were cynical and suspicious.

I love verse 4. "And Jesus, knowing their thoughts, said, Why think ye evil in your hearts?" That must have been something! They didn't even say anything, but Jesus answered what they were thinking and indicted their evil hearts. Their evil attitude toward Jesus proved that they didn't love Him, because if they loved Him they would have thought the best about Him. You see, in the case of hate like this, even though they couldn't find any faults in Him, they kept on looking for them. Why? Because once you start hating somebody, you'll try to find faults. Conversely, once you start loving somebody, you'll start covering their faults. That's the difference love makes.

Love is a harbor of trust for those who are doubted by everybody else. And as soon as somebody wants to get things right again, love is quick to restore the fallen brother (Gal. 6:1). You say, "But, John, what happens if you throw a mantle over a fallen brother's sin and believe that he's going to get straightened out and come back to the Lord—and he doesn't come? And what do you do when your faith begins to fade because you thought he'd come back?" A parent with a wayward child says, "Well, I thought she would come back to the Lord, but it's been fifteen years." Or the Christian wife with a non-Christian husband says, "I thought he would become a Christian, but I just don't know anymore. I don't know if he'll ever believe." What does love do then?

N. Love Hopes All Things (v. 7c)

"[Love] hopeth all things."

1. Hope's object

When you run out of faith, hang on to hope. Hope is the long line, the long cord, that never gets disconnected. As long as the grace of God is operative, human failure is never final. What I always go back to is this: Is anything too hard for God? I think back a few years to people that we've disciplined in our church because of various sinful situations. At the time, there was a great desire in my own heart, because of love, to throw a mantle over their sin and never talk about it or discuss it with anybody, except with those who were involved in praying for them. And then there was a great desire in my heart to believe that something would change—that they'd come back. And I guess in a couple of cases, now, my faith has gotten a little small. So do you know what I do? I hope. And every once in a while, when the long rope of hope pulls at my heart, I pray for them and keep hoping.

2. Hope's optimism

You see, love is hopelessly optimistic—it never stops hoping. Love says, "God is still God, and He can do it; so that's what I have to hope in." Love refuses to take failure as final. God wouldn't accept it from Israel, Jesus wouldn't accept it from Peter, and Paul wouldn't accept it from the Corinthians. Many a loving wife has held on to a husband with nothing but that rope of hope. Many a loving parent has held on to a wayward child, and many a loving friend has held on to a fallen brother—just holding on to hope.

3. Hope's obstacle

When all your faith gets clouded in, you have to hold on to hope. Don't give up on hope—love doesn't. You might say, "Well, I've lost faith in them totally. They're completely lost. They'll never come back. There's no hope left. I give up." Well, love doesn't give up on hope. That would be like arriving in a village beneath the Matterhorn in Switzerland on a foggy day and having people say, "You've got to see the Matterhorn on a sunny day. It's the most beautiful sight you've ever seen." Now, if you sat on the ground and said, "Liars, there's no Matterhorn. I'm right here, and I can see that there's no Matterhorn," you would be wrong, wouldn't you? But in that foggy moment, you thought you made a clear judgment. Love doesn't do that. When faith gets clogged up and fogged in, love still hangs on to hope. When doubt and despair steal faith, love still has hope.

The Determined Dog that Didn't Despair

In a large city airport, there's a dog patiently waiting for his owner to return. His master got on a plane and left him there—

over five years ago! Given food and water each day by people at the airport, he patiently waits in the same spot hoping that his master will someday return. Now, if the attachment of a dog for his master could produce that kind of faithful hope, certainly love could produce it in us if we really loved.

Love, you see, doesn't run, bail out, and leave as soon as the first mistake is made or the first sin is committed. Love waits and waits. And there are enough promises in the Bible to make hope work. You say, "But, John, if you bear all things, and you believe all things, and you hope all things, but the rope keeps getting further and further out, so that you feel that you're losing hope—then what do you do?"

O. Love Endures All Things (v. 7d)

"[Love] endureth all things."

1. The term explained

The Greek term translated "endureth" in verse 7 is a military term that has to do with being positioned in the middle of a violent battle. The emphasis here is not on handling little, minor annoyances. It's referring to love that stands against incredible opposition—and still loves.

2. The term exemplified

a) The apostle Stephen

When Stephen was lying on the ground with his life being crushed out with stones, he said, "Lord, lay not this sin to their charge" (Acts 7:60b). He wanted to throw a mantle over the sins of his people. He believed and he hoped—he preached with the belief that some would listen, and he hoped that they would come to Christ. And when he ran out of faith and hope, all he had left was endurance. As they were stoning him and crushing out his life, he was simply enduring, wasn't he? Why? Because he loved them.

b) The Lord Jesus

On the cross, Jesus threw a mantle over His crucifiers' sin, believed that some of them would believe, hoped that they would come to Him, and endured in the end, while they spit on Him, with the words, "Father, forgive them" (Luke 23:34a).

You see, love never dies. You can't kill it. It never fails. Even when that love for a wayward child continues year after year, and you get back hatred and bitterness and rejection, you never stop loving—you endure. That's the crescendo of love.

Love bears all hurts, wounds, sins, and disappointments; covers them with a blanket of silence; feels sympathetic, redemptive, and even bears the pain, if it can. Love believes the best about somebody, is never cynical, and is never suspicious—in spite of the way it's been wounded. And when love's believing is betrayed, love turns to hope, because God is still God, and He can do anything. And even when hope grows thin and all hope seems lost, love endures. It endures the deep hurt that seems so final with a triumphant confidence that the God who gives His children peace is still on the throne. You see, love is never overwhelmed. It cares too much to give up. It will die caring.

Tragically, there wasn't any love in the Corinthian church. They were like the church that Reinhold Niebuhr spoke of when he said, "The church is like Noah's ark. If it weren't for the storm outside, we couldn't stand the stink inside." But that isn't the way God wants it. He wants us to be characterized by love and the church to be a community of love. He wants to see these principles of love in operation.

Conclusion

A. The Fact of Love's Importance

You say, "John, I know now that love is important. It's important because it brings spiritual and physical wholeness, and it's important because it's characteristic of our Lord Jesus Christ, whom we are to manifest to the world. Now that I see what it is, what it does, and how it behaves, how can I begin to see God's love manifested in my life?"

B. The Five Keys to Love's Implementation

1. Acknowledge that it is a command (Rom. 13:8-10)

2. Agree that you have the power (Rom. 5:5)

3. Understand that it is normal Christian behavior (1 John 4:7-10)

4. Realize that it is the Spirit's work (Gal. 5:22)

5. Practice it (1 Pet. 1:22, 4:8)

Did you know that even Jesus learned obedience (Heb. 5:8)? We're to practice love. Start in your own home. If we put these fifteen characteristics of love into action, the world will look at us and say what God wants them to say: "Oh, how they love one another!" And that will exalt Christ.

Focusing on the Facts

1. How do we know that sin has certain effects? What two categories do these effects fall into (see pp. 97-98)?

2. What Old Testament passage dramatically shows us that continued unconfessed sin in the life of a believer has physical consequences (see p. 98)?

3. What is the connection between emotional trauma and physiological problems? How does that relate to a Christian sinning (see pp. 98-99)?

4. How was the sin in the Corinthian assembly affecting the believers (see p. 99)?

5. All sin is violation of _____ (see p. 99).

6. What is the greatest commandment? Why? Give scriptural support (see p. 100).

7. Why doesn't a Christian have an excuse to not practice love (see p. 101; cf. Rom. 5:5; Gal. 5:22)?

8. How do we know that Paul was using hyperbole in 1 Corinthians 13:7 (see p. 102)?

9. What is the basic meaning of the word "beareth" in 1 Corinthians 13:7 (see p. 102)?

10. When Paul defined love as bearing all things, what sin was he addressing (see pp. 102-3)?

11. Why do people always seek to uncover the skeletons in somebody else's closet? Why is this not to be characteristic of Christians (see p. 103)?

12. What does 1 John 4:10 mean when it says that God sent Jesus "to be the propitiation for our sins" (see p. 104)?

13. Love that bears all things: _____ someone else's sin, _____ with someone else's sin, and _____ for someone else's sin (see p. 105).

14. Explain what Paul means by describing love as believing all things. What are some practical applications of this quality of love (see pp. 105-6)?

15. What kind of effect do you have on people when you believe the best about them (see p. 107)?

16. How do we know that Job's "friends" didn't love him (see p. 107)?

17. When we begin to run out of faith, what is the long cord that we can hang on to (see p. 109)?

18. How does hope differ from faith (see p. 109)?

19. What does the Greek term translated "endureth," in 1 Corinthians 13:7, refer to (see p. 110)?

20. What are the five keys that will allow us to see God's love manifested in our lives (see p. 111)?

Pondering the Principles

1. In Psalm 32:3-4, we discover that David experienced physical consequences because of sin in his life. Then in verse 5, we read about how he finally dealt with it: "I acknowledged my sin unto thee, and mine iniquity have I not hidden. I said, I will confess my transgressions unto the Lord, and thou forgavest the iniquity of my sin." Can you think of a New Testament equivalent to this verse on how we are to deal with our sin? What's the best way to guard against the effects of sin in

your life? Commit yourself to take inventory of your attitudes and actions at the end of each day. Confess your sins and then ask God to show you the areas in your life that need to be worked on and improved. This type of daily spiritual accounting will keep you from suffering from the debilitating effects of sin.

2. On page 101 is a list of nine New Testament injunctions to love. Look up each of these verses, and then choose one of them to memorize and meditate on.

3. What is your first reaction when another Christian sins against you? Be honest! Is your first response to go to that person and confront them with their sin (Matt. 18:15), or do you rush to tell someone about what they did? How does love react? When someone comes to you with a juicy piece of gossip about another Christian's sin, do you discourage them from spreading the gossip, or do you encourage them with listening ears? Strive to love one another by covering one another's sins with silence. Now this doesn't mean that sin isn't to be confronted, it simply means that it is not to be broadcast to others. In fact, realize that gossiping is a sin, too, as it is a lack of love.

4. Do you talk about the faults and sins of your marriage partner or members of your family to others? If so, recognize that you are violating the character of love that covers a fault with silence. Ask God to help you become more aware of those times when you verbalize the faults of those closest to you—those to whom you have the greatest responsibility to love.

5. Read 1 Corinthians 13:4-7, and review the meaning of each of the fifteen qualities of divine love. Which of these do you have the most problems with? Write them down and put them someplace where you will be reminded of them daily. Realizing the importance of love, as it fulfills the whole law, commit yourself to concentrating on the practice of love.

6. On page 111 are five keys to implementing love in your life. Look up the references to each of these points. Then sometime today, get on your knees and say, "God, I know that I'm commanded to love. I agree that I have the power to love. I understand that it is normal Christian behavior to love. I realize that it is the Spirit's work to love through me. So help me to practice love."

Scripture Index

Genesis

3:5	55
49:10	32

Numbers

24:15, 17	32
25:1	32
31:8	33
31:16	32

1 Samuel

20:17	57

2 Samuel

12	98

Job

21:27	107

Psalms

32	98
69:9	87

Proverbs

8:13	68
10:12	103
11:2	68
13:10	68
14:30	53, 55
16:18	68
27:4	56
29:23	68

Isaiah

28:11-12	17
29:24	15
32:4	15
53	104

Jeremiah

1:5-10	34
1:16-18	34, 35
4:19	35
8:18-19	35
9:1	35

Daniel

3:16-18	41

Zechariah

4:6-7	38, 39

Matthew

5:44	27, 52
5:45	27
7:21-23	33
9:2-7	108
11:25	36
11:29-30	52
13:11	36
17:20	38
20:28	58
21:21	38
22:34-40	99-100

Luke

7:36-50	70
15:28	56
18:11-12, 14	40
23:34	50, 58, 110

John

3:16	10
3:30	68
8:50	58
12:49	65
13:1, 4-5, 34	10
15:9-10, 13	10-11
17:4	58
21:15-19	11

Acts

1:15	13
2:1-11	13-14
2:6, 8	15
5:1-11	99
7:60	50
10:44-46	16
11:15-17	16
17:16	81
19:6	16
20:19	35

Romans

2:4	50
4:6	84
4:8	84
4:22	84

5:5	101, 111
5:8-10	27
8:26	20
9:2-3	35
13:8-10	100, 111
13:10	46

1 Corinthians

3:3	55
4:6-10	66
4:18	66
5:1-2	67
5:1-6	86
6:1-8	82
8:1	37, 67
11:29	99
12	6, 7
12:10	16, 17
12:31	7, 55
13:13	8
14	6, 7, 17
14:1	101
14:4	72
14:7-8	14
14:12	72
14:18	13
14:21	17
14:23	18
14:26	64
16:14	101

2 Corinthians

2:4	35
5:19	84
6:6	49
8:8	101

Galatians

5:22	49, 111
5:22-23	7
6:1	108
6:2	73

Ephesians

3:3-6, 9	36
4:2	49
4:15	31
5:25	9

Philippians

1:9	37, 101
1:12-18	55
2:2	101
2:2-6, 8	12

Colossians

1:26-27	36
2:2-3, 9	36
3:14	101

1 Thessalonians

3:12	101
4:9	101

2 Thessalonians

2:7	36
3:5-6, 14-15	88

1 Timothy

1:5	100
3:16	36

Titus

3:4	52

Hebrews

1:7	20
5:8	111
10:24	101
13:1	101

James

2:23	84-85
3	88
3:14-16	56

1 Peter

1:22	111
2:3	52
4:8	46, 101, 103, 111

2 Peter

3:9	50

1 John

4:1	102
4:7-10	111
4:8	46
4:9-11	11
4:10	104

2 John

6-11	91

Revelation

2:2-4	41-42
2:4	8

115

Moody Press, a ministry of the Moody Bible Institute, is designed for education, evangelization, and edification. If we may assist you in knowing more about Christ and the Christian life, please write us without obligation: Moody Press, c/o MLM, Chicago, Illinois 60610.